They'll Teach You a Lesson

by
MaryAnn Aikins

authorHOUSE™

1663 LIBERTY DRIVE, SUITE 200
BLOOMINGTON, INDIANA 47403
(800) 839-8640
WWW.AUTHORHOUSE.COM

AuthorHouse™
1663 Liberty Drive, Suite 200
Bloomington, IN 47403
www.authorhouse.com
Phone: 1-800-839-8640

AuthorHouse™ UK Ltd.
500 Avebury Boulevard
Central Milton Keynes, MK9 2BE
www.authorhouse.co.uk
Phone: 08001974150

First published by AuthorHouse 3/2/2006

ISBN: 1-4259-2214-7 (e)
ISBN: 1-4208-7732-1 (sc)

Library of Congress Control Number: 2005907323

Printed in the United States of America
Bloomington, Indiana

This book is printed on acid-free paper.

Foreword

What did you learn in school today? Have you ever been asked that? I ask myself that every day and my answer always reveals that I learn something new everyday.

I began writing this book as a catharsis after a particularly challenging school year. I wanted to analyze what actions, of mine and the children's, may have caused what I felt was an disappointing year. I wanted to make sense out of what seemed to be a frustratingly wasted year. In that process, I reflected on many children over the years with whom I have worked. It was then that I realized I had learned a valuable lesson from each and every child over my 25 years-plus career in the field of child development/child care. All along, I was under the hallucination that I was the teacher, but realized we are all more than life-time teachers, we are all life-time students.

Robin Sharma, author of many books, stated that "Children come to us, more highly developed than adults, to teach us the lessons we need to learn." I couldn't agree more. I am grateful I have been in positions which allowed children to come to me and teach me valuable lessons.

Each chapter is dedicated to one child and the lesson he/she taught me. With the exception of my god children, Hannah and Noah, and Kerry in Chapter eleven, all the children's names have been changed. I find that using him/herself, he/she, etc. is cumbersome, so I have used the pronoun which identifies with the gender of the child highlighted in that particular chapter when speaking in generalities.

Thanks to my parents for the title. As I grew up, they frequently repeated the mantra of, "It will teach you a lesson." I didn't appreciate that phrase when I was young, but now I see the beauty and importance of it. Why else are we on this great Earth than to learn lessons? We only stop learning when we die, or we close our minds (which to me, is a living death). To live our lives fully is to embrace the eternal, perpetual change; and hopefully, learn and grow every step of the way.

Every time I see the father of a friend of mine, he asks, "What did the kids say today?" He loves to hear the amusing stories that invariably come from being around children. This has been helpful to me because it has reminded me that even on the worst days, there is always something to smile about. This has also inspired me to write some of the stories.

Whether you are beginning on a new journey, or have been around the block a few times, I hope this book will motivate you. It may even give you some tools and strategies to deal more effectively with all the people in your life, especially the young people. Maybe this book will be a way to take a few simple steps to discover and change what hasn't been working for you. Or you may just be entertained and inspired. Either way, I hope you enjoy reading about the children who have made a difference in my life.

Working with children has entertained, inspired, and fulfilled me in both my career and personal life. It's a mutually advantageous interchange because it has improved the quality of their life as well as my own. I've enjoyed the success of producing immediate and lasting change in the lives of children and their families, and you will realize after reading this book, they have done the same for me. Working with children can be demanding, but I demand more of myself than anyone else does. Part of that demand keeps me trying and learning those lessons. You will see I have quoted many other authors and resources. I have found their wisdom useful in my search for answers and I wanted to pass it on.

A good indication that you are learning from children is that you are still smiling, laughing, enjoying and being assured your efforts make a difference. If you aren't feeling this, remember a quote from Eileen Caddy, author and co-founder of the Findhorn Foundation states, "When you feel that you have reached the end and that you cannot go one step further, when life seems to be drained of all purpose; what a wonderful opportunity to start all over again to turn over a new page." I hope the pages of this book helps you find purpose and opportunity to start whatever it is you need to do.

In passing along some tips of the trade, I have gained from my experience. I hope you can gain valuable insight. Perhaps you'll even learn a new lesson. It's an honor and a privilege to be provided with experiences from which we can learn a lesson.

Peace and laughter,

MaryAnn.

Acknowledgements

Wendy Cook, for your wonderful editing and support. Thanks for making my work look as good as possible.

Joe Schwartz, for your encouragement and input. Thanks for reading all my rough drafts and believing that I am skilled and talented enough to complete this goal. Thanks for being my number one fan and coach, personally and professionally.

Shirley Graff, thanks for your early editing and for cheering me on every step of the way.

Ladina Bachman, for all your help when computers challenged me. You are my Swiss savior!

Stefan Berger, for providing me with a place to stay that was away from the hustle and bustle of my "normal" life so I could concentrate on my book and complete it.

Steven Lowman, for loaning me your laptop. I would have been lost without it. Thanks!

Janie Hess-Gray, for reading all my rough drafts and encouraging me chapter by chapter. I really appreciate your perspective.

To all my friends and family who lovingly put up with my determination to complete this tribute to the many people who have influenced my life.

And as always, I must thank all my angels who gently pushed me to keep working especially when I was doubtful.

Thank you. I love you all. I am SO blessed to have beautiful people around me no matter where I go.

Chapter One

Hannah and Noah

Hannah and Noah taught me – When you look at life through the eyes of a child, you will see it's the simple things that count.

It's a shame we grow up. I don't mean physically or mentally, but spiritually. Adults too often forget to see the beauty and wonder that is all around us everyday. Like the simple magic of "knock, knock" jokes. Don't ever assume listening to each and every one of these seemingly senseless rhymes is going to be a waste of time. Just yesterday, while talking with my godson, Noah, on the phone he said, "I have a knock, knock joke for you." Then he proceeded with, "Knock, knock." I probably answered half-heartedly, "Who's there?" He captured my whole heart with the unexpected punch line, "It's Noah, and I love you." I would never have wanted to miss that. It's simply beautiful and wonderful. It's what counts!

Even though Hannah and Noah come from a financially privileged home, they are still typical kids who prefer to play with the boxes in which toys came packaged. They find hours of simple enjoyment with rubber bands, trinkets, stones and good, old-fashioned marbles. And, of course, if you give them soapy water and a couple dishes, they could be contented for an entire afternoon because the whole world is a wonderland to them.

As we age, we tend to forget to stop and smell the flowers in this wonderful world of ours. Children know that the constantly changing universe offers an abundance of daily beauty and wonder. Adults tend to think nature is just something that is going on around us. Children come together with nature and embrace the discovery of what each and every new day has in store for them. It is simply magical how a child is drawn to connect with nature whenever possible. Typically, the first recognizable drawings of a child reflect the connection she has with nature. The sun in the right-hand corner, and a house in the center of the page, adorned with flowers on either side of it, maybe a dog and some birds. Children are intertwined with the beauty and wonder of nature. They are not a separate entity from it, they are a part of it.

Hannah's appreciation of the treasure trove nature has to offer was never driven home to me more than the day a little friend came to Hannah's house to play. The friend wanted to play with Barbie dolls and a playhouse. But Hannah was ecstatic over a toad we had found about an hour earlier. The other girl tried in vain to entice Hannah to play with manufactured toys, but Hannah was too intrigued by her toad. I even offered to take them to the movies, but nothing was as appealing to Hannah as that toad. After all a movie is one dimensional, a toad is real!

When I lived in my country house, some of Hannah and Noah's favorite activities were jumping in mud puddles and climbing stone piles and hills. We'd throw stones down the bank and gather sticks. And of course, find the elusive, precious toads. The excitement and pride of finding toads cannot be purchased in a store. Trips to the parks, indoor playgrounds, and store-bought gifts also paled in comparison to my sister's city-raised grandchildren when they visited my country home. One of their most memorable activities was burning the paper trash. It's the simple things. It's the basics. It's being a kid. It's simply wonderful!

One day Hannah and Noah were intensely involved in the yard for about a half hour. I glanced out the window every time I passed by. After finishing some household chores, I walked out to see what had occupied them for such a period of time. It was wild onions. They had pulled several dozen out of the ground and were filling the bucket of a toy dump truck with them. I don't think I have ever seen a toy keep their interest for that long, But nature can! With nature, imaginations soar and senses are filled. There's no directions to follow. It doesn't need batteries. You don't have to learn to use nature. You don't have to wait for it. It's always there and always changing. Nature can be explored and appreciated by oneself or with others. The possibilities are limitless. While interacting with nature, children learn how the world works, and how they work. It offers a free, boundless education.

One day, Hannah found a caterpillar outside. It looked as though it hadn't breathed life for several days, if not weeks. Hannah insisted it wasn't dead and asked if we could make a little house for it and bring it inside so it could warm up. I indulged in this seemingly futile but humanitarian effort by helping to supply it with a cardboard house and a little plastic dish for water and tissues for it's bed and blankets. She watched over that bug like a mother hen over her chicks. Well, I could not have been more surprised when we saw that little bug start to move. Hannah's excitement was wonderfully contagious. I was so proud of her efforts and happy for her accomplishment. I've never seen her excitement over an opened store bought gift match or even come close to matching the thrill she demonstrated over that one caterpiller.

What a shame we stop allowing ourselves to experience the abundance of simple pleasures. Through the eyes of a child, every button on a coat is examined, every grain on a piece of wood is studied, and endless amusement is enjoyed simply by sucking spaghetti through one's pursed lips. Adults need something as monumental as Niagara Falls to catch their attention. A child can appreciate the endless patterns of rippling in the water caused from a single drop of water, especially if he is the one who caused the ripple. Have you ever had the joy of watching a child fill with pride when he can demonstrate for you a new skill? Skills we take for granted as adults, such as, zipping one's own coat; pouring one's own drink; reciting one's own phone number; hopping on one foot; spreading butter on a piece of bread, riding a bike without training wheels. Mastering skills is an abundant pleasure to a child. Children don't need motivational tapes to guide them to set goals. They just embrace life and all it has to offer along the way.

Children would never miss the opportunity to stare at a sunset or sunrise and witness its magic. Raul Jimenez, a Cuban MD, prescribes, as part of his treatment plan for all his geriatric patients, for them to go outside for at least 15 minutes and stare at the sunset everyday to absorb the different rays of light thus letting go of their suffering, allowing them to enjoy the peace of the moment. Children do this everyday and they don't need some doctor telling them to do this. They just know it is there, so we should look at it and savor it.

Allow the child within you to come out and play a little every single day. I think adults should have fun designs on the bottom of their shoes and light-up shoes too, just to remind us what we thought of the world when we were seven or eight. And speaking of feet, can you imagine not minding stepping on an egg on the floor, but instead finding its texture to be irresistible? In fact, kids go out of their way to step on any gooey, icky substance that is within 10 feet of them. Their curiosity and impulsiveness outweighs inhibitions. Just once, experience the charge from playing with children, wearing all the wrong clothes, getting down and dirty just because it's fun. Children don't want to wait to have fun. They want to seize the moment, no matter what they are wearing. They don't see restrictions, they see possibilities.

A friend e-mailed me a beautiful sentiment about how children appreciate the little things in life and how we tend to forget to do this when we grow up. The e-mail states that: "when we see dandelions, we see a bunch of weeds. Kids see flowers for Mom and blowing white fluff you can wish on. When I look at an old drunk and he smiles at me, I see a smelly, dirty person who probably wants money and I look away. Kids see someone smiling at them and they smile back." Do we have to loose all our sweet innocence as we age? Do we have to become cynical and hardened? Can't things be just as they appear and not over analyzed or over complicated sometimes? Children see the world through untarnished and unmolded minds. Their inner voice of judgment never comes into play or alters their innocence. The one time this is evident is when I ask children to describe what they see in a series of inkblots. Their perception is so unique and fresh.

I received some cute quotes from children that describes how they perceive simple things through their eyes: "Clouds are high flying fogs." "Rain is saved up in cloud banks." "A blizzard is when it snows sideways." "A hurricane is a breeze of a bigly size." "It is so hot in some places that the people there have to live in other places." "The wind is like the air, only pushier." "The law of gravity says no fair jumping up without coming back down." "Rainbows are just to look at, not to really understand." "Someday we may discover how to make magnets that can point in any direction." "Most books now say our sun is a star. But it still knows how to change back into a sun in the daytime." "A vibrations is a motion that cannot make up its mind which way it wants to go." Think about what they are saying. This simple childhood logic makes sense! While hiking one day, I pointed out a woodpecker hole in a tree to Hannah and Noah. A few yards later, Noah pointed out a, "Hole pecker." He also titled a grasshopper a "jumping grasser." I like his words better. Then one day, Noah injured his neck at school. His dad, a chiropractor, took him to his office and administered electric stimulation on the muscles in his neck. When Noah first experienced the tingling feeling he described it as, "a thousand ants giving you a massage." It is such an accurate description, that now his dad explains it to patients that way when preparing them for their first treatment.

The appreciation of the little things in life starts the moment one is born into this vast world. Take, for example, how an infant endlessly looks at his own toes. Adults haven't done that since the 60's and that was drug induced, not true discovery! If a baby could talk, he would say, "What a strange world I have entered." He is eternally curious trying to make sense of it.

That is one reason why children go through the "Why?" stage. You know the one that drives all adults crazy! Can you imagine being so fascinated with your surroundings that you want to know every little detail about it? That must be wonderfully overwhelming. But then we get accustomed to the world and that's a pity because that's when we loose our enthusiasm. The world becomes just a matter-of-fact. We loose the ability to be astounded. That's probably one reason why adults struggle with so many problems.

When I was encountering a struggle in my life's journey, one of the books I read was, <u>The Spontaneous Fulfillment of Desire,</u> by Deepak Chopra. In that book, he writes, "As children, we tend to think of the future as a clean sheet of paper upon which we can write our own stories. The possibilities seem endless and we are energized by the promise of discovery and the sheer pleasure of living immersed in so much potential. But as we grow up, become adults, and are "educated" about our limitations, our view of the future becomes constricted. What once lifted our imaginations now weighs us down with dread and anxiety. What once felt boundless becomes narrow and dark." The possibilities are still there. We have been taught to restrict them, but we can be taught to rediscover the possibilities, too. If you need help, watch a child. To a child, everything is possible. To a child everything is simply wonderful.

I appreciate the insight of great philosophers, but children's philosophies are the best. A good philosopher has the ability of amazement and children definitely excel in this. Robin Sharma, author of many books, including the <u>Monk Who Sold His Ferrari</u> , tells a story that is a great example of how simple children can make what we consider to be complex: "A father was busy reading the newspaper one day. His little boy kept pestering him to play. The father, unfortunately, didn't have time to play with the little boy. The little boy kept asking over and over again for his father to play. Finally, the father tore a picture of a globe out of the paper and ripped it into many pieces. He told his son, "Here! Go put this together;" thinking it would take the boy quite awhile to do it. Well, the son brought it back after only a minute. The father asked, "How did you do that so fast?" The little boy simply explained, "On the other side of the globe was a picture of a person. Once I got the person together, the world was okay." Simple solution. Simple philosophy. Simply brilliant!

Since the Federally funded program, for which I'm employed, was on the chopping block last year, our state promoted a letter writing campaign to block this proposed action. In support of this action, I decided to have my students dictate letters to the President of the United States. One child stated that she really likes school and wants it to stay open. I asked her how we could get the money to keep it open. She responded, "Just go to the store, and they'll give you money because every time my Mommy gives them money, they always give her money back." Through the eyes of a child............

Children's eyes live in a constant state of discovery, adventure and unconditional love. I had a wishing well at my old house. We walked past it thousands of times a year and never thought a thing of it. But there hasn't been a child, who has visited there, who could resist turning the handle to make the bucket ascend and descend. They don't do this once or twice but several times. That's what it's there for, right? Through this seemingly contrite activity, a child learns how much strength it takes to move the handle; what happens if one lets go too quickly; how many times it spins before stopping; if you roll it tighter, you will have a different result and on and on. I never knew all this about my own wishing well. I just knew it needed a fresh coat of stain every spring.

At school we arranged orange cones in our gross motor room. We instructed the children to steer their tricycles around the cones. I needed to determine if they had mastered this skill for their assessment. Didn't they understand that? It was quickly apparent they didn't know and didn't care. They just wanted to ride. Well, only one child maneuvered her bike around the cones; the rest of the children discovered it to be more fun to crash into the cones. When I saw the first child do this, I said to my teacher aide, "I know adults who would do that." Then I realized how much more fun it must be to plow down the cones instead of negotiating around them. I have to admit that it is a fantasy of mine to drive on a local 4-lane that is frequently adorned with orange cones and mow them all down with a truck. Remembering this, I dropped my initial reason for setting up the cones and let the children plow them down. At that moment, I lived vicariously through the kids, because only kids can get away with that.

I have also lived vicariously, over the years, through my god children. One example of this is when I have encouraged them to paint and express themselves creatively. We have enjoyed this activity since they could crawl. They have preferred to paint in underwear so they wouldn't be constricted by the "keep the paint off your clothes" expectancy. Since they didn't need to be worried about where all the paint landed, their bodies were often covered in paint. Some marks were intentional and some were accidental. Either way, I had to use my own imagination to figure out a way to clean them without their painted feet walking or me carrying their painted little bodies through the house to the bathroom. I enlisted the aid of a basin of warm water on the kitchen floor. It wasn't long before they discovered that they could sit in the basin. That was fun, especially when water splashed out; which led to our discovery that the floor was slippery when wet; which led to our invention of "butt-naked skidding!" The bare-naked kids would push each other to get started and then they would slide across the wet kitchen linoleum. They usually crashed, feet first, into the refrigerator. I had as much fun watching as they had participating. They would slip and slide for at least an hour. Then I would dry them and carry them upstairs for their bath. I had explained this activity to their parents, who laughed at the thought of it. It also verified for them that I am quite weird. One day, their dad came home for lunch during one of our skidding escapades. As he was holding his side from the pain of laughing so hard, I said to him, "Be honest. You'd love to be doing that, too. Wouldn't you?" I think he blushed as he but admitted, "Definitely!" I know I would love to have tried it. Rachel Louise Carson, writer, scientist and ecologist who wrote several articles to teach people about the wonder and beauty of the living world stated, "If a child is to keep alive his inborn sense of wonder, he needs the companionship of at least one adult who can share it, rediscovering with him the joy, excitement and mystery of the world we live in." We didn't strip of our clothes to join them but we did join in their excitement and enjoyment.

I've been told that one of the keys to success in life is to rekindle the child within us and to express ourselves through that part of us that is most creative and least constrained by the educated and conformed mind. That is one reason why I would like to try the big blown up balloon things at fairs and carnivals. I always wanted to be allowed to get in one and jump around. But I can't. Because I'm "grown-up." One reason I love being a preschool teacher is because it enables me to still play with play dough. This stuff is great. If you haven't played with it lately, you should. Or just sit on the floor and scope the room. It takes on a whole new meaning from this height. Experience what the world looks like through the eyes of a child. Little things take on a whole new meaning.

Chapter Two

Ben

Ben taught me- seeds may take a long time to root but that doesn't mean we shouldn't plant them.

When Ben was about two years old, his mother remarried, which meant Ben and his two older brothers were under the rule of a new male figure. Twin girls were subsequently born to Ben's mother and stepfather. It was soon apparent that these girls were favored, and they regularly received preferential treatment as the years passed. The boys' clothes were purchased at Goodwill, while the girls were clothed from J.C. Penny's. The girls received regular dental and medical care; the boys were, sometimes, taken when they were really sick.

Daily, the dad degraded the boys, calling them awful names and making fun of them. Rules and consequences were so inconsistent that the boys had no idea what was expected of them and what was right or wrong. On the other hand, the girls could do no wrong. They were lavished with all kinds of privileges, deserved and undeserved. The only thing the boys were lavished with was a backhand or a slap on the back of their head. This could occur even while they were sitting quietly at the table doing homework. The dad would paddle them with belts, switches, hands, baseball bats, badminton rackets, whatever was nearby when he became raged.

When Ben was about ten years old, the dad threw a hammer at Ben and the claw part stuck in Ben's calf. The cowardly dad was afraid to seek medical attention for the injury because he didn't want to be suspected of child abuse. The wound became infected. He reasoned, in his warped way, that it was Ben's fault the wound became infected, so he would just have to live with it. "Good for him!" the dad was overheard saying. That was when my husband and I stepped in. We sought medical attention for Ben and supervised the healing of the external injury. Knowing the emotional damage was much deeper and would take a lot longer to heal, we offered to let Ben come over as much as he wanted and hang out. Ben's parents loved the idea. It was one less kid with whom they had to deal.

Ben's first step toward healing his emotional scars and building his self-esteem came when we took him to the barber and, at his request, had his hair spiked. The glow on his face was blinding. He looked in the mirror endlessly. The second was when we gave Ben responsibilities around the house and rewards for doing them. Helping us in our home remodeling projects provided Ben with the sense of being grown up and accepted. It was very important to him that a male role model trusted and believed in him enough to let him do adult tasks. The positive attention and feedback he received for his performance was icing on the cake. Ben began to open up and his confidence grew daily.

An article by Lou Manfredini, a home improvement guru and author of two books, states that ".... the satisfaction I see in my kids' eyes as they help me, whether it's a task as complicated as changing a faucet or as simple as hanging a picture, makes the effort worth it." I know what he means. When Ben assisted in some chores, it made "helping" take on a whole new meaning. At times it would have been easier to do it without him but seeing his excitement and pride assured us it was worth it.

In our continuing efforts to help Ben gain pride in himself, we bought him some new clothes. I would have to say this helped because he sauntered and paraded past the mirror until bedtime. Ben's ability in the art field was already shining through. We searched for outlets for him to develop that talent and receive positive reinforcement for it. In the book, <u>The Practice and Theory of Individual Psychology,</u> Adler declares that "above all else, people want to think that they count. The urge to create, to build, to be of use is strong in us." We wanted to help Ben find that strength in himself. It was going well.

School was ready to start and we offered to keep Ben and let him attend the school near us. His parents wouldn't agree to it. I honestly think they were jealous of how Ben was blossoming from the opportunities he was experiencing. Sometimes, when people don't feel good about themselves, they don't want to see anyone else feel good, either. They don't want to see others succeed because they feel they can't. It's easier to drag someone to a lower level than pull oneself up to a higher level. Maybe they felt threatened. For whatever reason, they wanted Ben back.

We kept in touch but saw Ben sinking into the abyss of the downtrodden. His good spirit and soul were in him but were getting pushed further inward as he had found he could get attention by doing undesirable actions rather than being a "good" boy. His older brothers were going down that path and Ben followed. Soon, Ben was flunking out of school, not caring for his appearance, and getting into petty trouble with the law. Nathaniel Branden, a pioneer in the field of self-esteem, writes, "The person who has no confidence in his own ability all too often allows someone else to run his life. It is rare that anything positive comes from that." Unfortunately, Ben was proving that to be true. I frequently thought if we had been able to help him build more self-esteem, he would have had enough confidence to run his own life. Too many of his needs were being neglected to enable him to trust his own mind.

The most important seed we can plant in children is self-esteem. Nathaniel Branden writes regarding children's self-esteem, "There is practical importance in developing self-esteem in your children when they are young. As we grow and develop, we continually face challenges of one kind or another. A child or adult who believes in his/her own personal resources is far better situated to live life successfully than a child who is inhibited or paralyzed by self-doubt and self-distrust." It doesn't matter what income bracket a child grew up in or if the parents stayed together or divorced; a child can be successful if they feel good about who they are. In the book, Stop Thinking Start Living, Richard Carlson states, "No one is born sceptical or negative. Self-doubt, self-criticism, negativity and pessimism are the result of negative thoughts that you have learned to take seriously. Your self-image and personality are a compilation of thoughts that you have about yourself, some of which may be negative." Those thoughts are planted in you. You are taught to have a low self-esteem.

Rather than teachers, parents are supposed to make their child feel like he is the most important and special child in the whole universe. Instead, families too often are individuals existing in the same house attending to the daily chores of the household. This is not the same as "being" with your kids. We should spend some time each day really looking at the children and not just looking past them. Children seem to be saying, "Look into my eyes, until you see my heart, and then I think you'll see that there's a special part of me, that you've never seen before." It's only when we look into their hearts, that we can truly say to them, "I think you're special, just because you're you." These words could have made all the difference to a kid like Ben. Jim Rohn, motivational speaker, philosopher and entrepreneur, stated,

"If you talk to your child, you can help them to keep their lives together. If you talk to them skillfully, you can help them build future dreams." Isn't that what it's all about? Children are and always have been mankind's only resource or future. Handle them wisely. They are the living messages of our life. What better way to plan for the future than to plant seeds in our children? It's not in vain. Whitney Houston sings "The Greatest Love Of All." A portion of the lyrics are, "I believe the children are our future. Teach them well and let them lead the way. Show them all the beauty they posses inside. Give them a sense of pride to make it easier." Beautiful song, necessary sentiment. We wanted to give Ben a sense of pride so his life could be easier.

Unfortunately the responsibility of planting seeds and nurturing children often falls into the hands of the school system. No wonder it's so hard to teach reading, writing and arithmetic. And what good are those skills to someone who feels he can't amount to anything? How can a child learn when he just wants to feel important for 15 minutes or when he just needs a hug? Learning is a challenge and no one takes on challenges unless they feel safe and secure. Life is one big challenge. It is one perpetual lesson. How can a child feel confident to try when facing a demanding task when he receives only 12 minutes of interaction a day from the most influential person in his life?

One day when I saw Ben, he was in tears. When I asked him why, he explained that his dad hit him because he was riding his bike on the road. I asked why he was riding his bike on the road when that didn't seem very safe. He answered, "Because yesterday, my dad told me I was allowed to ride there. I didn't know I wasn't allowed to today." Common situations like that creates a character full of self-doubt, self distrust, and low self-esteem.

Ben had no idea what was okay and what wasn't because the family rules changed with the unpredictable moods of his dad. He tried to constantly guess his dad's reaction to each and every situation, right or wrong. I'm sure the dad isn't able to predict his own reaction, so how can a child foresee it? Ben lived in a constant fight or flight mode, always ready for the worse.

Dr. Phil, psychologist and author, frequently states, "Children need to be able to predict the consequences of their behavior with absolute certainty." Children shouldn't have to consider what emotion is directing the decisions of the adult in charge. Not that we can precisely predict how anything will impact little minds, but we can sure sit back and think before reacting to anything they say or do in any particular instant. People like Ben's father get caught up in a spiral of centering everything on themselves and losing the love for others by focusing on himself. They don't make bad parenting choices to purposefully damage a child, but irreparable damage and negative impacts result none-the-less.

So, another precious seed that needs to be planted in children is the gift of consistency. Consistency builds trust, and trust makes a kid feel safe. A kid who feels safe will accept discipline better. It's a win-win cycle. It's a shame this cycle is never started with some kids, and broken with others. A study by a University of Michigan Health System team states that creating consistent routines will help promote better sleep patterns. This is important because the study showed that "young teens whose preschool sleep habits were poor are more than twice as likely to use drugs, tobacco or alcohol." A multitude of reasons exist to establish and reinforce consistent routines, guidelines, and rules.

My husband and I lost direct contact with Ben but through community connections or the local paper we heard that he was into drugs and had been in and out of jail throughout his late teens and early twenties. Once in a great while he would call from jail and try to explain his predicament. It seemed like he was trying to con us more than express true remorse for his actions. We sometimes heard that he didn't have a place to live. I wanted to take him in because I always had a soft spot in my heart for him, but my husband felt we had to remain disconnected and hardened or Ben would use us and take us down with him. Deep down I never gave up hope that Ben would remember the nurturing with which we showered him and how good that felt. Nathaniel Branden also writes, "It's an old adage that effective parents give children roots to grow and wings to fly. Every child needs the security of a firm base and the self-confidence to leave it one day." I hoped we had given him firm, healthy soil on which to grow.

I realized, when I heard from Ben about a year ago, that something must have taken root. He finally turned his life around at age 29. He has a son of his own and is living in upstate New York working as an artist. He thanked me for helping him, guiding him, and believing in him even when he didn't believe in himself. Way to go, Ben! I am proud of you.

As children, the quantity of choices available are limited. They expand as we mature and grow into adults. However, the quality of those choices are subconsciously driven by our childhood environment. That's why I thought it important to help Ben shift conscious attention to the quality of his choices as well as the seemingly infinite quantity available to people today. This change in his attention would inevitably allow him to become a better person and serve others in a higher capacity.

"Nurture the grass and it will grow. Don't just kill the weeds." I repeat this quote many times to myself when I have a challenging child in my class.

Do we see only weeds when there is grass in there too? Help the grass take on better roots and it will push out the weeds. Nurture the good in each child, and in the end, you'll see a beautiful garden. Iyanla Vanzant, author and inspirational speaker, wrote, "Few of us are taught that within our beings are millions of seeds of potential. Our thought patterns and emotional responses germinate those seeds that ultimately grow into experiences." Those experiences grow into who we are. Deepak Chopra in his book <u>The Spontaneous Fulfillment of Desire</u> states, "I believe that your thoughts, your intentions, are the equivalent of that light, and the world itself grows in a direction to meet those intentions." I wanted to provide Ben with an internal dialog that could support the intentions of his inner light. Carl Junge, a Swiss psychiatrist, is quoted as saying, "The curriculum is so much necessary raw material, but warmth is the vital growing plant and for the soul of the child." A void of love and acceptance blocks the soul which blocks learning. A child must be socially and emotionally fulfilled to allow learning to take root and to be a productive, responsible adult.

Deepak Chopra, also the author and founder of the Chopra Center for Well Being, states, ".....a seed has within it everything it needs to become a tree, the flower, and the fruit." Every child is a fragile seed that deserves to be nurtured so it can bloom and grow. To encourage that, we need to provide a fundamental base and fertilize it with strong values and morals. This will enable them to reach for the light when faced with darkness and come through it stronger and heartier and able to pass on these good traits. There is a Chinese proverb that goes something like; it is better to have planted a tree 20 years ago but planting one today is better than not at all. Never miss the opportunity to plant a seed.

Ben called me again New Year's Eve. He stated he fondly remembers the nurturing I gave him. Rudolf Steiner College believes that "we fundamentally affect the miraculous growth that takes place in the earliest years of childhood and our influence lasts a lifetime." They are remiss in mentioning that the influence of a child lasts a lifetime, too. I marvel and am eternally grateful for the growth Ben has provided me. He taught me to plant self-esteem seeds early and water them daily. All the other beautiful seeds will then flourish around it and soon you will have propagated a whole field of beauty.

The secure, positive seeds we planted in Ben was strong enough to enable him to breakaway from the negative cycle and turn the pain inflicted upon him into strengths. Keep growing, Ben and plant a few seeds along the way yourself!

Chapter Three

Max

Max taught me – I have to be in control of my reactions.

The challenge of Max came very early in my career for that I am grateful. I thought I had a lot of patience, until I met Max.

Max had severe autism with extreme hyperactivity. His sleep was limited to five hours a night. He couldn't sit for longer than three minutes. The transmitters in his brain confused the sense of pain and pleasure. It was not uncommon for him to dig at a small scrape on his hand until it was a gaping, open wound. It was common for him to catch bees so they would sting him. He would also hit himself frequently. Once he even pulled out a couple of his teeth during the night. To address these and other problematic behaviors, an intense behavior modification plan was designed for him at a children's hospital. I was to model implementation of the program for the parents and monitor their execution of the program. I thought I was adequately and effectively meeting the demands of this challenge, until one evening.

I was fortunate to grow up in a home where hitting was rare. For me hitting as a means of punishment was not a knee-jerk reaction. This was crucial on this milestone evening in my career. I was character. I was providing respite, for Max's parents to take a much-needed break. Bath time arrived. Being very kinesthetic, Max really enjoyed a bath. He would stay in the tub for hours, if allowed. After about an hour in the tub, I gave Max a ten minute transition warning that bath time was ending. He screamed at me. This was a common response to any unfavorable request. I ignored that inappropriate response.

After five more minutes, I gave him a five minutes warning. Again, he screamed, to which I gave no reaction. When I gave him a two minute warning, he screamed as he flung water at me. I stated, " No! You are angry because you have to get out of the tub, but bath time is over in two minutes." Two minutes later, I pulled the stopper to drain the water. Max spit on my face. I held his face to facilitate eye contact and sternly told him, "No!" and explained that if he did this again, he would sit in time-out. This was a customary method of modification included in his behavior plan.

Max smiled at me, then leaned over as if to hold on to the side of the tub and get out, but instead he bit me. I instantly felt a burning sensation run through every vein and muscle in my body. Instantaneously, my stomach tied in knots. Without conscious thought, I raised my open hand to the side of my head. It was only then that I realized my intent. Stunned, I slowly and deliberately lowered my hand. I looked at my hand, I looked at Max and thought, "I can't believe I was going to slap him."

Recognizing that I needed time to sort out my feelings of anger and embarrassment, I walked out of the bathroom. I knew Max would be safe in the bathroom by himself for a couple of minutes because the water had drained out of the tub. I stood in the hall, surprised at how this incident had affected me. My heart was beating hard and furious. I felt warm all over, especially in my face. My breathing was fast and shallow. I was plain sick to my stomach. I disliked the symptoms my body was experiencing so much that I vowed to never let my emotions get out of hand when dealing with a child again. I reminded myself that Max didn't do this to me personally. He did this because he is a kid and at the time, an angry kid. Max, like many non-verbal children, was impulsive and became extremely frustrated when he couldn't verbalize his wants and/or needs. I knew how important it was for me to work on my coping skills, so I could teach Max how to develop his own coping skills. I could react, or I could choose how I wanted to respond to this situation.

Bernie Siegel is a physician who has cared for and counseled innumerable patients. He also travels extensively to run and speak at workshops, sharing his techniques and experiences of dealing with life's difficulties. He offers a prescription for living that gives effective and healthy ways of dealing with the adversity that occurs in everyone's life. I have had the privilege of hearing Bernie Siegel speak at two different seminars. One of his strategies for living is to think about how someone you admire would handle a situation then strive to model that precedent. He always asks, "What would Lassie do?" A spin off from the inspirational Christian saying,

"What Would Jesus Do?" I frequently ask myself what would a person who I admire do in a situation like this?

I have had many wonderful role models throughout my career. My goal is to take pieces of each of them and form them into me. I know many people who would have hit Max. In fact, a lot of people would say, "All that kid needs is a good swift kick in the pants." The ironic thing about this situation is that Max would have been pleasured if I had hit him-just another reason why reacting physically would have been wrong and wouldn't have taught Max anything constructive. Remember, autism confuses pain and pleasure. I don't know if this knowledge was controlling my reactions that evening or if someone from above was holding my hand and controlling me. Whatever or whomever it was, I am eternally grateful.

Hitting is never the answer. One of the most ludicrous things I witness is when a child gets hit for hitting or gets yelled at for yelling. It is obvious how the child learned this in the first place. An upset dad told me his son had hit him. He couldn't believe it! He told me he sternly instructed his son to never hit him again. I asked, "And did you tell him that you will never hit him again, too?" The dad looked at me with confusion and embarrassment. I suggested that this boy has been hit, especially when his parents were at the end of their rope. I asked if the boy was frustrated at that moment when he'd hit his father. The dad reflected and answered, "Yes." I replied, "Well, that's what he's been taught to do when he feels that way. Why would you expect him to act any differently? Have you taught him any other ways to handle his frustration and anger?"

I once had a Mom tell me, "I spanked him until his butt was red and he still didn't listen." I asked," What else have you tried?" She looked stunned and said, "What else is there?" I don't know what people think they're teaching their children by hitting them, but hitting only teaches hitting. I've never heard about or seen a calm, controlled parent spank his/her child. Adults spank children out of frustration and fear. They fear they aren't in control. Adults reason that inflicting pain on this little, trusting child who weighs one fourth of the adult's weight, will establish control. The misleading illusion in spanking is that it appears to correct behavior. It can produce immediate desired responses. The child does stop the behavior the adult is addressing-for the moment. Unfortunately, in the long term, spanking is damaging and ineffective. The purpose of punishment and discipline is to teach a child skills of self-control so he can conduct himself properly whether a parent is around or not. If the only skill he has learned is hitting,should he go around hitting himself to go in self-control? Spanking does not teach self-control or self-correction. I heard an ironic story not long ago of a mom who stopped her van three times within three miles to hit her children because of the children's misbehavior. My thought was, "Didn't the mom figure out on the second stop that spanking was ineffective since she had to do it again, especially in such a short period of time? Why didn't she try something else?" It reminded me of that old saying, "Insanity is doing the same thing over and over and expecting different results." Einstein said, "You can't solve a problem with the same insanity that causes it."

Think of it this way. You have to attend a business meeting. Since you aren't feeling very well, you decide sitting by the door would make a quick exit, if necessary, less distracting. When you enter the room, you see someone else sitting there. You need a minute to process this and change your thinking. While scanning the room, your boss enters and instructs you to sit down. You begin to explain about your desire to sit near the door. She hits you! Does this make you feel like sitting anywhere in that room? Does it help work through the process of figuring out the next best place to sit? Do you think hitting a child helps him adjust his gears to the next decision? This may seem like a ridiculous example because adults wouldn't do that! That's the point. I have seen adults do that to children; and since it isn't appropriate with one adult to another, why is it okay to do to it to a child? It is not a skill the child needs to learn since it is not one he can use to function in society. So why teach it?

While cleaning out my mother-in-law's belongings, my husband found the old metal spoon that his mom used to hit her kids. He reminisced about how all the siblings could hear the spoon rattle on its handle as she ascended the stairs shaking it. He said they all jumped in bed as fast as could. I thought, how sad to threaten children with bodily harm to make them appear controlled. Children don't learn from being fearful of their parent. They learn more effectively when they have mutual respect. I think about the teachers who had the greatest impact on my learning. They weren't the ones whom I feared, it was the ones that treated students as people rather than something to control and feel powerful over. Fear is a distressing emotion. It causes fright or apprehension, panic, trepidation and anxiety. It may be valuable when under attack or danger, but is counter-productive to learning from and trusting the adult with whom they love. Carl Jung is quoted as saying, "One looks back with appreciation to the brilliant teachers, but with gratitude to those who touched our human feelings." Not one teacher who has touched me with bodily harm learned my respect.

Since my husband grew up learning that to discipline is to hit, he would hit our first boxer dog when the dog was disobedient. After a couple years, my husband saw that when he raised a hand for any reason or moved too suddenly, the dog would cower. This broke his heart. He realized that all he trained our dog to be was afraid of his master. He vowed to never hit an animal again. Since then we have had many pets. The relationship between man and pets has been mutually rewarding. They trust him and know the only thing they'll ever sense from him is love and hugs. He feels much better about it and I'm sure his pets do, too. They fearlessly obey him now.

Ever since my revelation while dealing with Max, I remind myself that I am in control of my feelings and actions. I consciously decide how I want to react. Nobody can make me feel anything. Only I can do that. Max may bite me but it is me who decides to be angered by it or not. A friend of mine recently asked me how I can always seem to be so well balanced and even tempered. I responded, "It's a conscious choice." When I'm feeling angry I stop and try to determine the real reason behind my anger. John Gray, author and speaker, states that behind anger is always fear. So I analyze why I am afraid. It's often a very painful realization but revealing. All this enlightenment hasn't given me all the answers, not by any means, but I can't help observing that people who hit children are always acting out of the fear of not being in control of the child. Most people feel the opposite of fear is courage. It isn't; love is. On the other side of fear is freedom. I choose to be free of fear. So when I'm feeling fearful of a situation, I approach it with love and am always amazed at the results. That's when I'm really in control. And if I'm not in control of my own emotions, how can I even begin to help a child be in control his? Controlling one's reactions is a win-win situation for all involved.

Chapter Four

Hannah

Hannah taught me -to choose my battles.

Hannah is my goddaughter. I love her immeasurably. She can be difficult at times, though, yet I wouldn't have her any other way. One reason is because her obdurate ways has helped me learn to loosen up on control when it doesn't really matter. Hannah is the typical strong-willed child who wants what she wants when she wants it and she wants it NOW! This can mean that Hannah doesn't necessarily want purple socks, but if the suggestion of blue socks is made, she'll fight to the finish for purple socks. She may even put on blue socks once she feels she has won the verbal battle.

I discovered early on that every issue could be a fight for control with Hannah, if I would feed into it. To avoid this, I let her think she is making the choice and thus getting her own way. Issues are resolved more quickly and quietly this way. I found if I give her two or three choices, such as, do you want to wear outfit A, B, or C, it benefits both of us. I can still practice some control in the important areas, such as making sure the outfits suit the occasion or the weather; and by selecting among A, B, or C, she has made a choice. This has another benefit too. If later she decides she doesn't like her choice, she can't blame me! Maybe she'll even consult me the next time!

Of course since kids will be kids, sometimes they don't like any of the choices offered and resort to manipulation. For example, one night Hannah was dilly-dallying instead of attending to the task of preparing for bed. Her brother, Noah, had already completed his routine, so I rewarded him with some celestial stickers, which he enjoyed putting on a piece of paper and taping to his dresser. When Hannah walked in, undressed, she expressed that she, too would like some stickers. I said in an agreeable tone, "Okay. As soon as you put on your jammies you can have some." She demanded them right then. I reminded her she had the choice of controlling when she received her stickers; it could be now, if she put on her jammies promptly, or it could be later, if she delayed getting dressed. It was up to her. Well, she didn't like those conditions and began to cry. She should know by now that I've seen many crocodile tears in all my years of dealing with children. But Hannah, being a typical child, tried this method of manipulation for herself. I calmly pointed out that her crying was only delaying her gratification, and all she needed to do was choose to get dressed. If I would have given in to her during her crying time, she would have learned that when she wants something from me, all she has to do is cry. This wouldn't do her any favors because it just doesn't work that way in the real world. This is setting her up for hardship in the real world. When Hannah saw her crying wasn't affecting my position, she chose to get dressed. She acted mad at me through the whole process. She wanted to believe that I had been unjust to her. She received stickers upon completion of the conditions just like I had told her. This whole process took about half an hour. To comply immediately and receive the desired incentive would have taken about three minutes. But then Hannah wouldn't be Hannah.

I remind Hannah frequently that her choices are up to her so as to help her avoid letting others make decisions for her. I also remind her that she is accountable for her decisions. It's important for children to learn to make choices and be held accountable for their actions and choices. It is a skill they will need daily for the rest of their lives. Adults make decisions everyday. It is a skill that has been learned, and confidence has been gained along the way. Nathaniel Branden, guru of self-esteem books, writes "*Parents also should remember that it is important to respect the child's need to struggle in the learning process. At one point or another, the parent may want to step in and tell the child the answer or show him how to solve the problem. But the fact that the child is wrestling with the learning process doesn't mean that anything is wrong. All learning involves some struggle. Part of the feeling of achievement that comes from learning is the sense of having tackled a problem and subdued it - of having won by virtue of your own efforts. The parent may be motivated by good intentions in trying to solve the problem for the child, but the parent is really aborting the child's learning process. Children need to know the extent of their own abilities - that they can overcome problems in the world, even if it takes a certain amount of effort."*

Sometimes choosing battles means letting a child experience natural consequences instead of controlling choices. I love natural consequences. If you aren't familiar with what these are, it's when a child insists on going outside without a coat, and once out, realizes that she is really cold. Guess what she'll do?.......she'll come in and put on a coat. So why get into a power struggle with whether to wear a coat or not. The child will get cold and find a coat, I promise! Natural consequences negate the need for a battle. Another good one is when a child refuses to eat. The natural consequence is she will get hungry; so she will eat. No battle - just time.

In other situations, common sense tells you to tackle a small battle now to avoid it snowballing into a bigger one later. There was a boy with autism in my class who repeatedly removed his shoes, especially when frustrated, which was frequently. I had to decide whether it was worth the battle to keep shoes on this kiddo at the beginning of the year while dealing with the demands of the rest of my class, or to ignore his shoe-less feet. But then I realized that if I ignored it now, I would be setting myself up for a bigger battle when I decided in three months I had time to enforce it. It is important to remember the long-term affects of ignoring some battles. Madeline Hunter heads an educational approach followed by many teachers. She explains, "For a child to unlearn an old behavior and replace it with a new behavior, you need to repeat the new behavior on the average of 28 times. So 20 times are to eliminate the old behavior, and eight of the times are used to learn the new behavior." "Nip it in the bud!" as Barney Fife, from the Andy Griffith Show, would say.

I'm frequently amazed at parents who seem genuinely surprised when their 14 year old is defiant and out of control. I can guarantee you this child didn't wake up one morning and say, 'I'm going to be totally different today. I have never been sassy, and it hasn't been modeled for me, but I am going to start today!' This kind of attitude has been developed and perfected for 14 years. Perhaps not consciously and not with the intent of becoming an obnoxious teenager, but through trial and error; through finding out what gets desired results and what doesn't, this personality style has formed. It's like a person who suffers a heart attack. The problem to the heart, which resulted in symptoms so severe that they couldn't be ignored, didn't start the night before during their sleep. Damage had slowly developed in their heart over years. It just became too severe to ignore anymore. If a child's problems are dealt with while they are developing, future problems will be prevented. It's like servicing your car routinely. There isn't anything wrong with the car every 5000 miles when you change the oil. But if you wait until 50,000 miles, trouble arises. Try fixing it then, if you even can! Sometimes it's irreparably damaged. Sometimes it can still be fixed but now it is going to take work on several areas instead of just one. One thing for sure, it won't fix itself, and it won't get better by ignoring it. Too often we deny the implications of a child's current behaviors by concluding that these problems are just a "phase." They will go away. Each stage and phase a child goes through represents the influences in her life. Behaviors could be a cry for help or a warning signal. Sometimes behaviors start as a phase but end up becoming a part of our personality. I have met people who seem to be eternally stuck in the terrible twos stage! While some things can be ignored and others shouldn't be, how situations are handled is the determining factor as to whether a behavior is a stage or a permanent part of someone's personality. The adult must make a conscious decisions to ignore a behavior or deal with it. Make sure you are choosing to deal with an issue, not battle about it. Sun Tzu, the name used by the unknown Chinese authors of The Art Of War states, "The best battle is the battle that is won without being fought."

Sometimes people set up situations which create battles. Take the following real-life story for example. After a day of shopping a mom brought home a new package of socks for her eight year old daughter and explained that she bought them for the start of school, which was in two weeks. She instructed her daughter to try them on. The daughter immediately said, "They look like boys socks" in the whiny voice she uses on her parents when she wants her own way. The mom pointed out that the ankle socks have pink on them as she tossed a pair to her daughter. The daughter reluctantly tried them on and whined that they weren't soft enough. It could have been any excuse. She just did NOT like those socks for whatever reason. Instead of respecting that or waiting until another time to reintroduce the socks, because this little girl's mood changes as quickly as the weather in Maine, the mom became upset and declared, right in front of her daughter, that she was NOT going to have this struggle every morning while getting dressed for school. She threatened that she was going to have to wake the little girl, who likes to sleep in, at 6:30 every morning to be sure she is ready for school. This just told the little girl what behavior was expected from her in the mornings. Chances are they are going to argue about socks, or whatever the topic of the day is, each and every morning. After all she just gave this child permission to behave that way with no incentive for behaving any other way. I'm sure the mom felt threatened by her daughter's defiance and growing need to be independent. But control is not gained by threats and battles. This set-up sounds like the makings of an on-going battle to me! I wonder who will win?

The sad thing is, neither will win. It is an endless battle just for the sake of perceived control.

Dr Phil warns, "You don't want to get into a battle with your child, but if you do, you had better win." Just for clarity, I need to point out these "battles" are verbal. In no way do I want to be interpreted as promoting physical battles. That is NEVER okay.

When you are yelling back at your child, are you in control? No, she is because she knows she is so powerful that she made an adult stoop to her level. She now feels invincible and armed. This leads to an unpleasant, disagreeable, distasteful, offensive, undesirable, embarrassing, and maddening situation for all involved. I doubt that is anyone's desired goal but that is what is achieved when you let a child take over. I once had a mom tell me, "I'm arguing with a 4 year old, and he's winning!" Some thing's got to change there. The parent has to gain control in a situation like that. Children just aren't yet equipped with all the responsibility that goes along with being in control. There is a great video by Dr. Thomas W. Phelan called, "1,2,3, Magic." It teaches parents how to stop an argument before it gets started. If you're battling with your child, do both of you a favor; get this video and implement the techniques.

In my classroom, one of my goals is to teach effective conflict management skills to the children so they can handle their own disputes without an adult running to their aid immediately. One time I do insist on controlling a situation quickly and consistently is when I see someone being bullied. Bullies are kids trying to negatively gain control over others. I have a zero tolerance for bullies. I insist on being the one in control in these situations for everyone's safety. One of the worst cases of bullying at the preschool level, I have witnessed, was from Artie and Zeek.

Artie and Zeek didn't know each other before attending my class. Artie was a leader and Zeek a follower who was trying desparately to fit in somewhere. Zeek didn't have other friends in the class. He had a difficult time with academics as well as social development. Artie picked up the required academic skills just by attending school. He needed no extra instruction. Their friendship bloomed by November of that year and soon after, discovered there is power in numbers. As is typical with bullies, they were compatible with their classmates when one of them was absent. But together the dynamic duo were nasty and hurtful and just plain mean. Their bullying behaviors included teasing other children, taking their toys and calling them names. I spoke to the parents of each child in the Nov. Conferences and voiced my concerns about how they are feeding off each other and conforming to peer pressure. I warned them that this could lead to their child making bad choices later in life due to peer pressure. I explained this is one of those things that can't be ignored or it will escalate to where no parent wants to go. Somewhere along the five years of life of these boys, the message that being domineering and intimidating was okay. Different methods of feeling powerful and competent needed to be instilled in these boys or they were in for a future on the dark side. It was important for these boys to find an adult authority figure who could display control in a manner they respected. I tried to fill that role but consistently received the messages that they, and their fathers, feel a woman is less respected than a man. My main goal became to protect my standards of no bullies allowed in my classroom. They paid a consequence each and every time I witnessed an act of intimidation. At least that way, the other children knew I was in control and insisted on a safe environment for all. I will not give up control in that area.

Something in their upbringing told Artie and Zeek that bullying is an accepted tactic to get what you want. Children start out as an empty slate. Each and every instance in their lives makes a mark on that slate. Each and every incident is impressing upon them who they are and what is okay in their family's value system. To better instill the morals and values of the family of my god children, I often give them the simple statement of, "You are a Schwartz. And Schwartz's just don't do that." This is appropriate at times when they ask me if they should smoke when they get older, or if I think they will ever go to jail. I want to impress upon them these behaviors are not within the moral guidelines of acceptable behavior in their family's belief system. Similarly, A teacher aid told me that her son was picked up for petty possession when he was a teen. After they paid bail to get him out of jail, he said, "No other Ringler has ever been arrested before, huh?" He knew that is just not okay in that family. That embarrassed him more than any words from the disappointed parents could have. He had to live with that knowledge. His parents didn't have to get into a lengthy battle with him because they had consistently impressed upon him that some things in that family are just not okay. Hopefully by instilling a strong sense of who they are, some battles with my godchildren can be avoided down the road. Nathaniel Branden writes on children's self-esteem, "Children do not grow up in a vacuum. They grow up in a social setting, surrounded by other people. Most of their early learning occurs through encounters with their parents, grandparents, siblings and others who come into the family circle." It's important to control who bears an influence in your child's life.

Sometimes the need for control is negated if we just listen. Nathaniel Branden: "One day, I was swinging my granddaughter around by the arms. This was something she loved. But at some point, she said, 'Let me down, Grandpa.' But because I was having so much fun myself, I continued to swing her. She said, 'Grandpa, you're not listening.' And I immediately realized that I wasn't and set her back down on the floor. By listening to what my granddaughter said, I treated her feelings with respect. A child who is not allowed to have a voice in what happens to him will not feel entitled to his own views as an adult. Often a child has a sense of being loved by his parents but not of being respected. Children become frustrated when they're not taken seriously by adults." If your child feels respected she won't feel she has to battle for control. She'll ask, if she knows you will listen and take her seriously. No battle for control is needed.

In the words of the Gambler, "You've got to know when to hold 'em, know when to fold 'em, know when to walk away, know when to run." This holds true when deciding whether you've got to loosen up the reigns or hold tight for control. Sometimes it's a gamble. Chances are if you have treated a child with respect, and have earned respect from your child, the control will be established and the battles few and far between.

Chapter Five

Daniel

Daniel taught me......the importance of setting limits and following through.

I saw Daniel and his mother for about 15 minutes one day while waiting at a doctor's office. After only about one full minute, Daniel's behavior, or rather his mother's, was making me consider waiting out in the car. But then I realized I was observing the perfect example of parenting that creates a child who ignores requests and disrespects authority.

The encounter started with Daniel going through his mother's purse; to which she requested, "Stay out of my purse." He ignored her request and continued until he found some breath fresheners. He triumphantly displayed his discovery and flashed his mom a huge smile. She rolled her eyes and shook her head as she told him, "Only one!" Okay, that was glaring error number one: He received a reward after disregarded the request to stay out of the purse. Daniel poured three breath fresheners onto the palm of his hand. His mom instructed, "Only one." He proceeded to slam all three into his mouth. She reacted by letting out a big sigh of defeat. He smiled! Then she instructed him to put the rest of the breath fresheners in her purse because if he were to eat more, he would get a bellyache. He held onto them. She ignored his noncompliance.

The mom and dad exchanged a brief conversation about the contents of a small brown paper bag the dad was holding, during which Daniel was being rambunctious and continually interrupting the conversation. The subject changed to a conversation about the mom's headache. Then, with

Daniel within earshot, the mom said, "I wonder how many headaches I'll get when he goes to school. Probably none!" And laughed. Daniel's attention seemed to still be on the brown paper bag. He began to demand to see the contents of the bag. Since my wait was occurring at an urologist's office, I suspected the bag contained a urine or semen sample. I was amusingly curious as to how they were going to keep Daniel out of this bag. He asked about 6 times, even used the magic, "please" word. Finally the mom said, "If you look in that bag, the doctor will come give you a shot." I moved uneasily in my seat at this point. Threatening a child with harm from a policeman, fireman, doctor or anyone like that is a definite no-no in my book. I wondered if they would connect the possible affects of this threat to Daniel's fright and tears the next time he has a doctor's appointment.

Daniel lost interest in the bag as he helped himself to more breath fresheners. His mom said, "Daniel, I really don't want you to have more of those. You'll get sick and then you will have to go to the doctor for a shot." Then she asked him to give them back to her. He quickly slid them into his pocket. She said, "Okay, but they have to stay in your pocket." I wondered if she really thought he would keep them in his pocket or if she said that in an attempt to continue hallucinating that she was in charge?

The nurse called Daniel's dad to go back to an exam room. Daniel wanted to go, too. Of course Mom threatened with, "If you go back there with Daddy, the doctor will give you a shot. Do you want a shot?" I almost laughed out loud when Daniel replied, "Yes, I don't care." I thought, that's right. A child doesn't really know what that means and even if Daniel does know, he has it figured out that his mom doesn't follow through with her threats, so he knows he isn't getting a shot.

Daniel's attention went back to the breath fresheners. I had the feeling he was realizing that Mom had control over whether he went with Dad or stayed with Mom, but he had control over whether he ate breath fresheners or not. For whatever reasoning, out came the breath fresheners from his pocket. He challengingly asked, "More?" Mom said, "NO! Your belly will get sick." Of course, Daniel helped himself to more then whined again about going back with Daddy. The mom, who was visually frustrated by now (Gee! I wonder why?), asked, "Do you want to go outside and wait?" Daniel replied, to his mom's apparent surprise but not mine, "Yes." So Mom took Daniel out in the hall to wait. I heard struggles about the candy going on out there, too. Then Daniel asked to see Daddy again and began to open the door to the office. Through the slightly opened door, I could clearly hear his Mom threaten, "Stay out here. You'll be in there all by yourself!"

What do you think happened? Yep, Daniel came in, pulled the breath fresheners out of his pocket and poured several into his mouth. Mom came in a few seconds later shaking her head at him. Thank God the friend, for whom I had been waiting, came out at that minute so we could leave.

This whole incident reminded me how important it is to set limits and follow through. Accomplishing this makes life so much easier for an adult/ child relationship. Dr. Phil, psychologist and author, warns parents who let their children control them, "You got the tail wagging the dog." This can't happen if you want to be effective parents. Setting limits and consistently enforcing them lets the child know up front who is in charge and what is expected of him. One benefit of this is that the child will monitor his behavior without the need of constant supervision. Attaining this is accomplished with common sense, respect and care. It cannot be accomplished with idle threats, outrageously threatening statements, or unrealistic consequences. I remember hearing one grandmother repeatedly tell her granddaughter that she couldn't go outside because the bears would get her. Why needlessly create fear in a child? Just tell her, "No!" and if the child still decides to go outside, give her a consequence to her poor decision. I turned a distant in-law into the child protective services because I heard he routinely used scare tactics to keep his son in bed at night. The dad hung scary masks above the boys bed and if the boy got out of his bed, the dad would put on a mask and make awful noises as he chased the boy back to bed. This is not an acceptable or effective way to set limits.

Neither of these methods is a good technique for teaching children to comply with and respect adults. I have learned that these tactics, not only waiver on the side of abusive, but aren't effective in accomplishing the ultimate goal. I don't use either of those tactics with children and have success in their compliance. One of the most common questions I hear from the parents after observing my classroom is, "How do you get them to clean up?" I don't do it by threatening or by becoming upset at their noncompliance. I do it by making it rewarding and fun for them. They don't even realize they are performing a task they really don't like. This is a skill that a child will draw on the rest of his life. There isn't one of us, on the face of this planet, that doesn't have to do things we really don't want to. For instance, who wants to go to work on the first beautiful day of spring? People who have learned to be responsible adults go to work even if they really don't want to so they can earn a paycheck and buy desired items. It's good to teach children that we all have to do less desired things in order to be able to do desired things. I teach children one of the best things you can do is make these chores fun and change your thinking about it. You will accomplish the task quicker and with a better frame of mind, if you do that. This is a great skill to teach children, that will benefit them over and over again for the rest of their lives. Dr. Maxwell Maltz, a widely known and highly regarded plastic surgeon and author of <u>Psycho-Cybernetics and Self-fulfillment</u> states, "In the household we find another battle between authority and freedom of thought: parental authority and freedom of expression for children. Discipline of a child must be creative, not destructive. Indeed, it is more a test of the adult than of the child. Understanding and self-respect are keys to creative discipline."

I also follow through with the consequences that I have pre-explained to the children. At the beginning of the school year, I give the children three chances to comply. With each request, I remind them of the consequences they will face if they choose to ignore our requests. Then, and here is the magic wand of avoiding endless frustration for you and helping children learn to comply, I follow through. I am as good as my word. Every time!

If a consequence is stated to a child, it is imperative that it is executed. This provides order, stability, security and comfort in a child's life. When a child pushes limits, it is really a cry for security, and reassurance that someone loves him so much that they care what happens to him and will protect him from harm. When a child thinks, "How far can I push the limit?" he is really thinking, "How much do they care about me?" Having no limits can convey an attitude of not caring.

I remember when I was 15 years old, a friend of mine had been invited to a party with her older boyfriend. She didn't want to tell her boyfriend, "No," because she feared he wouldn't like her anymore. But she was nervous about going because she knew there would be alcohol and drugs. She acted disappointed when her parents didn't permit her to go but was actually quite relieved that they loved her enough to set limits. Also, now she could tell her boyfriend that her parents didn't allow her to go, which took the heat off her with her boyfriend. Children want limits. They need limits. The benefits of setting limits are plentiful.

Keep in mind, consequences need to be age appropriate and the punishment should fit the crime. For example, when time-out is used as a consequence, the number of minutes a child sits quietly in time-out should be the same number as their age. That is age appropriate. And if a child accidentally spills milk, he shouldn't have to clean the whole house, or go to his room for the rest of the day. That is extreme.

It is important to set consequence you can enforce. It is ridiculous to threaten with, "You have to come straight home from school and go straight to your room, with no phone calls, TV, or computer for nine months!" You know you will back down from this, and so does the child. Or tell a three year old, no play dates for a month. First, after about two hours, he won't remember what he is being punished for and second, this may be extremely difficult to enforce. Or telling the child who forgot to feed the dog that you are going to get rid of the dog, all the while you and the child know that would never happen. It is an idle threat. And the child knows it. This does not produce compliance or respect. In fact it produces disrespect. The child learns he can just ignore the parent. The most common, unenforceable threat I hear is when an adult wants a child to come with him. When the child doesn't show an indication of being ready to go, the adult states, "I'm gonna leave you here!" The adult can't just leave a child and an older child knows it. However, it really puts fear into a small child. This creates a multitude of spin-off problematic behaviors. It's just not an appropriate or effective way of managing that situation.

The adult has to be prepared for consequences, too. I always warn, "Ask a question only if you can accept the answer." If a child doesn't have an option of cleaning up, it's not good to ask, "Do you want to clean up?" If he answers, "NO!" what are you going to do? After all, you asked. You gave him the choice! Now you have to deal with the consequence of his response. It is better to prevent that scenario. If the child truly doesn't have a choice, just request. Then if the child chooses not to comply, you follow-through with a reasonable consequence. I have found it is best to be specific when stating your requests. Such as, instead of asking a general question like, "Could you clean up sometime?" Be specific and ask, "Could you clean up before 5:00?" The child knows your exact requirements of perceived compliance and then if he chooses to ignore that request, you can follow through with an appropriate consequence.

If the examples of not setting limits weren't glaringly apparent to you in story of Daniel at the beginning of this chapter, read it again. It is no wonder this mom has headaches and is frustrated. She has taught Daniel to produce these results by not setting and enforcing limits. I'm sure that wasn't her intent but it is the result non-the-less. Setting and enforcing limits takes some extra effort in the beginning but the end result is worth it for all.

Chapter Six

Elliot

Elliot taught me - the importance of using positive statements.

Elliot was a kid who had learned he received the most attention when he acted-out in a negative manner. He and his four brothers, were being raised by their father. Sometimes his father had a paramour living with them, who had three kids of her own. Elliot's self-esteem was very low. He had already, at the age of four, been rejected by his mother. He wasn't developmentally capable of keeping up to his main role models, his older brothers, who were suffering from the same confusing anger from which he was apparently struggling. Elliot's anger reared its ugly head several times a day and almost assuredly at transition times.

In preschool, we assemble in a line to switch from one room to another. The recognition of another's need for personal space isn't yet recognized in most preschoolers, so they assemble very close to one another. Elliot seemed to perceive this close proximity as an invitation for touching others and the touching was not usually in a positive way. He would often push, hit, nudge, or pinch whatever his busy little hands could manage at that moment. In the beginning I tried reminding Elliot of the rules at school, but it quickly became apparent that he knew the rules. He also knew he was breaking the rules and, unfortunately, sometimes getting away with it because he had become skilled at doing his physical antics when he was certain I was preoccupied.

In the beginning, when he had displayed his uneasiness in an inappropriate manner, I'd put him in time-out. This usually enraged Elliot.

During his rage it was common for him to obliterate entire shelves of toys. He would scream and yell, kick and hit. Anger poured out of him until it dripped from an agonized expression on his face. When the anger drained from his body he would usually pitifully weep and exhibit shame. It was painful to watch, so I knew it had to feel much more painful for Elliot to experience. When time-out is used properly, it can be a very effective tool for some children. But not for Elliot. One size does not fit all when dealing with children.

The first time Elliot demolished the room during one of his rages, I called my supervisor for suggestions on appropriate ways to help him at that moment. I wanted to help him clean his destruction but what message would that send to him? Would I be conveying that it was okay for him to trash our room when he was displeased, and that I would always clean up his mess? Yet I knew this mess was too massive for any preschooler to tidy up. My supervisor suggested that while I helped him clean I express to him that I am helping because I care about him, and not because I will clean whatever mess he feels like creating. While we were cleaning, Elliot softened, and smiled at me, in a genuine manner several times.

This activity built trust and got us through that destruction zone but I realized this wouldn't help him gain self-control or self-esteem. In order to hold him accountable for his actions, I tried making him remain inside when the class went outside, but this was to no avail. After he showed his displeasure of this punishment by throwing anything within his arms reach, he would sit, almost contentedly, and smirk. Nothing seemed to help him learn to keep his hands to himself even though each time he was acting out in our line, I would remind him of the consequences of his physical antagonism.

Then one day, instead of reminding him he <u>couldn't</u> go outside if he pushed, I reminded him to keep his hands down so he <u>could</u> go outside. I realized that if I stated to Elliot, "You won't go outside if you push," he was working toward not going outside. He figured, "I can't do this so I may as well blow it now. And blow it big time! After all, she is expecting me to push!" He was validating the old self-fulfilling prophecy. He would get the stress of trying not to push and trying not to fail out of the way. It was easier for him to do that than to comply. It was also what he thought was expected of him.

I realized that I was expecting him to fail. I knew I had to think of a way to help Elliot feel good about himself and succeed. I discovered that if I just worded my demands in a positive manner Elliot responded positively. I also found that if I told him, "Don't hit," he had no idea what to do with his hands. So I instructed, "Keep your hands at your sides so you can go outside." Consequently, he knew just what to do with his hand so he could go outside. This thinking follows the old philosophy of what do you think of when someone states to you, "Don't think the color blue."? Automatically the color blue floods your thinking. Instead of telling him to not think of the color blue, I was telling him to think of the color green. Then he knew what was okay to go ahead and do. It provided him with a specific, positive direction on which to focus.

Elliot had a smile on his face the entire time in line because he knew he was going outside. I had a smile on my face the entire time because I knew I found a way to help Elliot control his impulsive responses. An unexpected plus was that I recognized I sounded much more pleasant and felt more pleasant too. I couldn't believe how well this rephrasing worked for all my students. Upon reflection I deducted that Elliot knew the consequences to his behavior. He didn't need to be constantly reminded, especially not at one of his most stressful times such as when he was standing in line. I'm sure to him it seemed like I was constantly reminding him, "You can't do it!"

The result of the power of expectations was exemplified by an experiment conducted in the Chicago school system. The researchers picked, at random, teachers and children. The teachers were told they were hand selected because of their proven ability to work with gifted children. After the teachers experienced success with these students, they voiced that they really enjoyed working with gifted children and would like to continue. They were then told that the children weren't gifted at all. They were also picked at random. The researchers called this result the "Pygmalion Effect." Since the teachers had high expectancies of the children, it helped the children believe in themselves and succeed accordingly. It is well documented in many instances that people rise or fall to the level of other's expectations.

A little change in my wording meant all the difference to Elliot. Instead of saying, "If you run in the bathroom, you'll have to leave." I'd say, "If you want me to stay here with you, you need to go to the bathroom and wash your hands and line up at the door" because step by step instructions helped him stay on target. I said, "a little change in words," but let me tell you it was a very conscious effort on my part to rethink every statement to be a positive one. I can't begin to count all the times I began a sentence only to rethink it to a positive statement which changed my initially intended direction.

It took a lot of practice, but it was definitely worth it for Elliot and every child I've since taught. When the children's behavior seems to regress, I rediscover that I am the one who regressed and must willfully remind myself to state my instructions in positive phrases. Kahlil Gibran, poet, philosopher, artist, prophet, and writer states: "Sayings remain meaningless until they are embodied in habits." I practiced until this became a habit. I learned about the "Collateral affect," which is a philosophy that reveals when you increase the good behavior, the bad decreases. I found a way to interpret bad behavior more positively. For instance, punching could be a child's only known way to connect with others. So the goal would be to help him learn to connect in a more appropriate manner, not to punish him for his attempts to be part of a group. Knowing this helped me realize that the problem I wanted to distinguish may actually be a solution to a much greater problem.

A child doesn't want to work toward a negative goal anymore that an adult does. How successful can a child be if he knows someone in authority is lying in wait for him to fall short? Children are happier, thus more productive, when they have something positive to work toward. The world doesn't always offer immediate rewards for doing what we're supposed to do, so if we have a built-in reward system, instilled in us as children, couldn't we cope better as adults?

This whole revelation reminded me of something a wise professor told me. He said that children hear visually. "What?" I asked. Then he further explained. When children are told, "Don't spill your milk." They visualize a glass of milk being spilled. But if it is stated, "Please keep your milk in the glass." As odd as that might sound, they visualize a full glass of milk remaining in tact. When instructed, "Don't run!" their little minds refer to themselves running and sends a picture, to their brain of them doing just that. So a request such as, "Please walk" works amazingly more effectively. State what you want them to do not what you want them to stop doing. (I have found this works well for adults, too.)

Professor Robert M. Williams explains that anytime a child hears a statement such as, "You're stupid/How many times do I have to tell you?/ You're lazy/You never have your homework done," a child has to battle with trying to overcome that person's negative opinion of him. I've learned it is more effective to tell children, "You are smart/You are a good listener/ You can accomplish anything." The proper use of Pygmalion Power is to say, "That's not like you! You're capable of.." And describe how you want that child to be as if he truly is capable of living up to that description. When I catch a child behaving in a manner that I would like to reinforce, I have learned it is valuable to say, "That's one of the things I like about you. You...." and describe his positive behavior to help him form an identification with it.

It was modeled for me at very young age to scrutinize others so it was natural for me to set-up Elliot and watch for him to be off-task. Unfortunately, since I was looking for it, I found it every time. I had been too swift and deliberate to point out his errors. This had to be very stressful for him and unfair of me. I had been too worried about being right instead of being effective. I viewed it as troubleshooting. Richard Carlson, author of <u>Stop Thinking Start Living</u>, states: "Troubleshooting is a socially acceptable form of mental illness. Many people are proud of their ability to predict potential problems, see fault in others, and remember past mistakes. They consider fault-finding skills necessary and important. Troubleshooters often raise children with low self-esteem. They are so busy pointing out ways that their children could improve that they totally forget to enjoy their presence. The children often interpret their parents' attitude to mean that they are not good enough." Since I don't want to do this, I now try to set kids up, and watch for them, to do right. I'd rather be fair so the children can be right. This revelation has made me declare that, in teaching and in other aspects of my life, to avoid saying the word, "Don't." It was an amazing powerfully negative word. Once conscious of it, it's amazing how frequently I was saying it. Did it get me what I wanted? Did it make me feel good? Did it make me more productive? Did it put me more in control? I don't think so! Thus, I learned that shifting my consciousness from avoiding a negative to pursuing a positive works better overall.

Chapter Seven

Lexi

Lexi taught me – Not everyone is a potential performer.

Lexi was a petite five year old. She lived with her grandparents, Nanny and Pappy, and saw her mom occasionally. She was surrounded by adults at Nanny's house, and thus was most comfortable in the company of adults. She began the school year glued to the leg of the assistant teacher or me. We were so pleased as we watched her gain enough confidence to leave our side and play with her peers. Although any conflict with a peer brought her right back to an adult's reassuring side, we thought, with us by her side, she had grown secure enough to participate in the school's performance before a crowd of parents and friends on the last day of school.

When I first began teaching, we had an elaborate graduation ceremony. The kids wore traditional caps and gowns and performed a skit and several songs for all their relatives. Some kids did great during rehearsal but froze during the real thing. Some kids just stood there, some kids held their hands over their ears and some would just plain cry. Eventually the agency streamlined a policy of a smaller production for the graduation performance because it wasn't fair to the kids who aren't comfortable on stage.

It turned out that even our downscaled graduation program wasn't downgraded enough for little, shy Lexi, though. She walked in with a high step and a smile on her face, until she looked around and saw all the people. She began to cry. I quietly talked to her for a bit and asked if she wanted to go give Nanny a hug then return to the stage. She nodded. I led her to Nanny and Poppy. They cuddled her for about 10 minutes then Nanny led her to the stage. Tears began to flow again before Lexi's little feet even hit the stage. I held her and asked if she could remain with us if I held her. She sobbed, "I want Nanny." I led her back once more. Her Nanny returned her just in time to receive her diploma. And Lexi smiled. That was enough for her.

Later, I explained to her disappointed Nanny that I could have made her stay on stage with us, but that would have just taught her to be afraid every time she had to stand in front of a group of people. It also would have taught her that the people she trusted, put her out there for the wolves to eat and wouldn't help her. I felt I had failed to prepare her properly, but then realized that all the other children did just fine. Lexi just wasn't ready for this experience and maybe never will be. Not everyone is a performer and that's okay.

Not everyone is conditioned to be somewhat comfortable in front of a crowd. My husband doesn't like a room with more than 10 people in it! He tells me of how frightening it was when he attended school to even think about rising for his turn in round robin reading. He said he was afraid the other kids would laugh at him. When he first regaled me with this memory, I was surprised to hear that not every kid wanted to be the center of attention at a young age and could be inhibited. Dr. Robert Ackerman, a professor at a local university and a renowned author of many books, tells a story from a child who stated that "reading out loud in class just made me hate reading." Often being forced to do something in which we're uncomfortable doesn't make us comfortable, only resentful.

A couple years ago, I attended a program in which my god children performed. One little boy stood with his face in his hands and cried through an entire song. I was upset that the teachers didn't try to help him or ease his fears in any way. They seemed angry that he was "messing up" their finely tuned program. They forgot that he was a child with individual needs, and they are supposed to be meeting those needs, not adding to them. After all, he wasn't reneging on a million dollar contract! He was just listening to his emotions- something adults tend to forget to do. Demanding this kind of performance is too much pressure on any five year old, let alone a shy one.

My childhood included lots of public performances. My first performance, at about six years old, was for the local Lions Club, singing, "Talk to the Animals." I remember being extremely nervous even though I had rehearsed it a thousand times. Prior to going on stage, I repeatedly told my oldest sister that I had to go to the bathroom. She took me the first couple times then explained to me that I just had stage fright. They wouldn't delay for my bathroom runs because the show must go on! The music began and soon it was my cue. I began to quietly sing, then, at the urging of my sisters and the smiles of the crowd, I was soon bellowing the words like a seasoned performer. When we were finished the applause was like a drug and I wanted more. A star was born! Hundreds of shows later, I still get a bit nervous at the start of a performance but soon glow in the ambiance.

Some kids enjoy performing. Some kids don't. We need to remember to let children dance to their own beat, even if it is the beat of a different drummer. Be sensitive to all personalities and help them find their niche. Maybe Lexi would be a great lighting person or sound person or costume person. It takes more than the people on stage to put on a show. It takes all kinds of talented personalities. And I hope I can help each child shine in her own spotlight.

Chapter Eight

Vinny

Vinny taught me — Each child is a unique addition to the class.

Vinny was admitted to our program the final seven weeks of classes. Until then, I had enjoyed a decorous class. Then came Vinny, a four-year-old bundle of rambunctious, unbridled, unstructured boy. Vinny's mom and dad were in their young 20's and had two more children younger than Vinny. Both parents had jobs that required them to work long hours. Vinny's grandfather often assumed the role of care giver.

When Vinny first started, he wore a red bandanna around his neck every day. Unfortunately the same milk spills and body fluids that were on the bandanna one day remained, and were only added to, the next day. I used gloves on the third day and removed the crud—infested napkin/tissue/whatever bandanna. I sent a note explaining the need for laundering it daily, if he wore it daily. We never saw the bandanna again.

Then there was the day Vinny arrived with a pocketknife. I promptly sealed it in an envelope and sent it home with a note explaining the danger of letting a four year old be in possession of such an implement. It was later explained to me that the Grandpa and Vinny often whittle while waiting for the bus and this particular day Grandpa forgot to retrieve Vinny's knife before he got on the bus.

I heard so many colorful stories about Vinny's grandfather, like when the bus driver reported to me that on at least three occasions, Vinny and Grandpa emerged from nearby trees when the bus stopped. They had been taking care of "nature," as Grandpa would explain. I didn't know what to expect when I made a required home visit to Vinny's house. I quickly found out to expect anything! After being there about three minutes, Grandpa declared, "Miss MaryAnn sure is pretty. Can I kiss her?" Vinny was embarrassed or feeling like my protector, I'm not sure which, but he slapped his Grandpa right across the face. I was ready to remind Vinny that we need to give nice touches and use his words to express anger when Grandpa taunted, "Come on Boy! Is that all the harder you can hit? Why that was no more than a fly slap." Vinny slapped him again and Grandpa laughed. (By the way, I made sure I maneuvered as far away from Grandpa as possible the remainder of my visit just in case he was serious about that kiss!)

Vinny's home environment spilled over into our classroom, causing havoc in my previously well-mannered room. He would kick, bite, slap and that was just when he stood still long enough to make contact. Otherwise, he frequently darted out of our room without asking, and wasn't able to sit and attend for longer than 20 seconds, even during lunch. I've been less active during a game of Ping-Pong than I was trying to keep Vinny in his seat during a meal. It was apparent that he'd never sat to eat a meal before coming to school. I was out of my seat redirecting Vinny more than I was sitting. I certainly didn't overeat those last seven weeks!

Also, when he wanted a toy, he wanted it NOW, and he would use any means possible to get it. Once he dragged a boy across the floor by the back collar of his shirt. The dragged boy was waving his arms and yelling, "Let me go!" It actually was a funny sight. Don't worry. I haven't totally lost it, yet. I knew the dragged boy wasn't being injured and I did quickly intercede and sat Vinny in time-out. After two weeks of feeling like Taz had been assigned to my room, and wondering just what I had done to deserve this, I designed a plan to help Vinny stay focused and obey the rules without involving drugs for him or me! Thank goodness, it worked. Talk about a transformation! Vinny made considerable progress in the following five weeks. But not a complete eradication of misbehavior. Vinny was still Vinny through and through.

It came time to start rehearsing for our graduation ceremony. To prepare the children for the upcoming event, I repeatedly explained to them about who may be watching them sing and every time, without fail, Vinny would ask, "My 'ad, 'oo?" I would respond in a variety of ways but he echoed the question every time we would practice. I started to ask the question just to hear Vinny ask his standard query. He was predictable in, at least, this area.

It was the last Wednesday of our school year, with only three days left. I read the book, <u>Don't Eat the Teacher</u>. For those of you not familiar with this fun book, it contains a repetitive text that I encourage the class to anticipate and cite. The class would always excitedly yell in unison, "Don't eat the Teacher" at the appropriate time. Then we would hear the delayed solitary voice of Vinny saying in his broken speech, "On'd ea da ea'er." He was on Vinny time! And I wouldn't have had it any other way. It was so cute.

Graduation day arrived! I really didn't know what to expect from Vinny when he saw all those people and I didn't know if his Dad was going to be there. During rehearsals, Vinny did great. He stood and sat when required, sang all the songs, did all the motions, and appeared to be having a good time doing it. But this was the real thing and although we had seen remarkable progress in his rampant behavior, Vinny was still Vinny. He was as good as Vinny could get but it still paled in comparison to the well-groomed behavior of the rest of the class.

Vinny came through as cute and endearing as ever. We sang our final song, which ends with the children shouting, "YEA!" and triumphantly raising a fist in the air. During rehearsals Vinny proved his own time zone by echoing "YEA!" after all the others had said it in unison. My wish came through. Vinny yelled, "Yea!" after everyone else and it was the piece de resistance! What a finale. Every trial and tribulation he had put us through the past seven weeks proved worth it in that one moment. And it couldn't have happened if Vinny hadn't bounced into my room the last seven weeks of school. That unique little guy kept bouncing until he bounced into everyone's heart.

Chapter Nine

Colby

Colby taught me- to love each child as if it were his last day.

Colby wasn't in my class but in another morning class in our school. He was a cute and wiry little fellow with one eye slightly crossed. He had a side smile that was sly yet loving. The harder he smiled the more you knew he loved you. He used this smile tirelessly, even when restricted to the time-out chair. Everyone in the school knew this infectious smile because often his teacher and aide would enlist the help of others in the center to help keep him on track. The previous year he had instantly fallen in love with a teacher aide. This aide wasn't married and Colby repeatedly told her that he would marry her some day. It took her about one full minute to fall hopelessly and forever in love with this little guy. We discovered he had that affect on everyone.

Then one day in early December, Colby's home tragically caught fire. As soon as the fire was discovered, Colby's mom cradled his little sister in her arms and grabbed Colby by the shirt as she raced for the front door. For some reason that no one on this earth will ever know, Colby jerked and pulled until he broke away from his mother's desperate grasp. She spent many life-threatening minutes frantically calling and searching for him but the intensity of the quick spreading fire forced her to retreat outside without her son. That turned out to be the last time she ever touched or saw her little boy. Once outside, she did the only thing she could do: hold onto the hope that the firemen could rescue him when they arrived. As excruciatingly long minutes passed, it became painfully apparent that all hope would be buried among the fast accumulating, charred rubble that was once a home to this little boy and his family.

Colby's teacher cried as she screamed in utter shock, "What?" upon hearing the news; after which she felt like she was falling even though she knew she was still standing. Word spread somberly through our staff. Silent tears displayed our disbelief. We couldn't speak. We just held one another and sobbed. I think each of us phoned a loved one, at one point, just to confirm their safety and to be reassured that our entire life hadn't just been turned upside-down. It was unbelievable the way the entire school was not the same because one little boy was taken from us. It was difficult yet therapeutic to walk in and face 17 other little people, who had been Colby's classmates, some of whom were already talking about the "big fire." It reminded us that life goes on and that we had to put the children's needs ahead of our own, now more than ever.

I had thought that losing a child due to the family moving was difficult but this was simply heartbreaking. How could one little 30-pound boy leave such a huge hole in our school? I couldn't even imagine what the family had to be going through. The feelings of loss, guilt, sadness, anger, disbelief, confusion, betrayal, and the endless second- guessing have to be unbearable beyond my imagination. How can so much life be snuffed out so quickly? Why that particular little boy? Why so close to Christmas? Why, why, why?

One reason I never had children is because my husband had felt, first hand, the unbearable pain of the loss of a little one from a fire. His two-week-old nephew, whose middle name was that of my husband's, was robbed from the world a few years prior to my entering his family. He explains that it's something you never "get over." He was so convinced that he could never stand the devastation of losing a child of his own that he was too afraid to take that chance. I could see some of that pain re-lived when I shared with him our disastrous news from school. I also know now that it is something you never "get over." It changes something inside of you forever.

Colby's early departure from this world taught me many things. One was to never take fire drills lightly. I had always stressed fire lessons in my classroom, such as getting out of a burning building and staying out; stop, drop and roll; and never play with matches, but I teach it with a precise conviction now. I re-thought my teaching strategies because I knew Colby had been taught those life-saving rules, too. I analyzed why he didn't heed those valuable lessons at that crucial moment. Then I tried to figure out how to teach so a child would better follow those instructions when needed.

It taught me that we are there for each and every child, not a class as a whole. It also taught me to love every child as though it were his last day. I don't mean morbidly, but because there are a lot of reasons that a child could be in my class one day and gone the next. It's easy to take those in our lives for granted, especially kids because they are healthy and resilient. This event helped me to remember that every day is important and that you may not get a second chance. I don't remember where but I recently heard the quote that, "What we do for ourselves dies with us. What we do for others lives forever." Colby is gone from our vision but he will live on forever in the lessons he taught us.

There is a boy in my class now who is being transferred to another center. This final week with him in my class has been so precious, as I remember that each and every day is precious with each and every precious child! Today is a gift. That's why it's called the "present." Love each day with each child for the present it is.

Chapter Ten

Noah

Noah taught me - It doesn't matter what my hands look like, it's what they do that matters.

Noah is my godson. He and his sister have been the inspiration for many chapters in my life. This chapter is about one aspect of how Noah's beautiful spirit positively affects me. I have never liked the appearance of my hands. Sorry mom, I have my mother's hands. My fingers are stubby and my knuckles are big and bulging. The veins on the backs of my hands are almost always popping out, and my skin is always cracked and dry. I have difficulty growing fingernails and the nail on the middle finger of my left hand is deformed from plunging it in a bowl of hot mush as I sat on my mother's lap when I was about one year old. My right thumbnail is rippled with ridges. Arthritis is settling in, so my index fingers are twisting and bowing. I hardly ever wear rings because I don't like to draw attention to my hands. I've always been critical of my penmanship and felt that my mundane handwriting reflected the appearance of my hands. As you can now tell, I am very conscientious and critical of my hands.

My perception of my hands has been reinforced out of the mouths of babes. Once a boy in my class, unbeknown to me, was studying my hands as I worked with another student. He actually said to me, "Why do your hands look so old when your face doesn't?" I think that was a compliment, at least that's where I put it in my book of self-esteem, anyway. Another boy asked as I helped buckle his seat belt, "Why do your hands look so ugly?" My opinion has been validated a few times. But not with Noah.

One of my favorite things in the whole wide world is putting my god kids to bed when I babysit them. It is such a special, cozy, warm ending to a day. We reflect on the happenings of the day and discuss plans for the next day. I know some of our communication is a stalling tactic on their part. I didn't fall off that truck yesterday! But I indulge in it because it is truly quality one-on-one time. Our routine is: bath, brush teeth, and three stories in Noah's room. The stories are an important step in our winding down process. An added benefit is the wonderful appreciation and enjoyment of literature the kids have developed from this simple bedtime ritual. After story time, it's lights-out. Noah likes the adult who is putting him to bed to lie with him for a short period of time. While his music plays softly, Noah carefully positions his Bubba along side his neck, and securely wraps his little hand around my right hand, which is resting on my other open hand. It is one of the most peaceful, relaxing, tender sensations my weathered-looking hands have the honor and privilege of experiencing. As we lay there, one evening, I was observing how beautiful Noah is; then as I continued to scope the serene scene, in the soft glow from his night light, I noticed how beautiful his hands are and amazingly, how beautiful my hands looked and felt wrapped in his. Noah was able to bring out the beauty in even my hands. How miraculous!!

Barbra Streisand recorded a great song about Grandma's hands. The lyrics talk about how Grandma's hands "ached and swelled," but Grandma's hands also, "picked me up each time I fell." The lyrics go on to tell of the wise wisdom those old hands had gained and distributed over their many years. At the end of the song, it says, "But I don't have Grandma anymore. If I get to heaven, I'll look for Grandma's hands." Barbra had a Grandma who taught her the importance of hands, and thankfully, I have Noah to show me the importance and inner beauty of mine!

The importance of hands is everywhere. Some of my favorite pictures are ones of an adult holding the outstretched hand of a little one as they walk along. I recently needed to go through my old college notes and found I had written many sayings on the front of my binders and along the margins. I rediscovered one of my favorite sayings from way back then: "If all the hands that reach could touch." I can't imagine not having the privilege of caressing the hand of a loved one, greeting someone with a hearty handshake, blowing a kiss, or waving a parting sentiment. The daily ritual of petting my animals is one for which I am repeatedly thankful. Having one's hand gently kissed by an admirer is always a gentle moment. It's one I've had the joy of giving and receiving. One of a parent's first fond memories of their infant has to be when he wraps his tiny little hand around one, seemingly huge finger of his parent. That touch can creates instant bonding, which transposes to instant love!

So many emotions can be expressed through our hands. They tremble and shake in good and bad times, they cover our face when we are embarrassed, and can be tightened into fists when angered. And the power of prayer is heightened when we fold our hands to God. That's the power of hands! The great Michelangelo knew the magical touch of hands as he displayed on the ceiling of the Vatican's Sistine Chapel, "*Creation of Adam*." Its simple beauty has withstood the test of time, and the unspoken message continues to touch many. Daniel Kettler wrote, "The touch of love in my own wrinkled hands will pass on to the hands of my son.........I want most of all when my son takes my hand, to feel that love lies in the grip." I feel that from Noah. I can only hope he feels my love for him, too.

When Noah was an infant, I repeatedly enjoyed watching him discover his own hands? It's wonderful how he was amazed at these extensions of himselves. He twirled his hands and moved each finger and gently swayed them, then furiously shook them. This caused him to gaze in awe and giggle incessantly. Wow! All because of hands. The fascinating discovery continues through childhood. I can't count how many times children in my classes have drawn around their own hand and felt great pride and wonderment. Some children repeat this activity endlessly. It's like their appreciation of their own appendage is eternal. Adults accept appendages as being a part of them instead of discovering them each day.

Hands are just like a person's overall appearance - it doesn't matter what they look like but what they do that matters. I don't like the outward appearance of my hands but I've also learned to be careful of what I take for granted because it could come back to haunt me. I've not appreciated the appearance of hands, but I appreciate that they have aided in the priceless connection between a precious little boy and me. I think of Noah every time I hear the inspiring song, "Reach out and touch somebody's hand; make this world a better place if you can." Thanks Noah, for making this world a better place and for showing me the importance of my hands. With you, they are simply beautiful.

Chapter Eleven

Kerry

Kerry taught me-Forget stereotypes and labels.

Kerry was a tiny, skinny little boy. His glasses were probably as heavy as his upper torso. Once you read his story, you'll understand his why he had a small stature and admire how strong such a little guy can be.

Kerry started out in this world only as big as his dad's hand, because he was delivered at only 24 weeks gestation. His birth weight was a mere 1 pound, 4.5 ounces. His mother, Deanna's, health had taken an unexpected ill turn during her pregnancy that made Deanna's chances of surviving risky too. She went into renal failure and her brain was swelling due to high blood pressure. At one grim point, her body was failing so rapidly that a nurse actually suggested that Deanna let her husband know her last wishes. All she could think was, "I just turned 23 yesterday." Reality was a blur as a priest came to give Deanna her last rites at the same time the ambulance personnel were preparing her for transport to a better-equipped city hospital. There wasn't a minute to spare.

Five days later they found they couldn't stop the inevitable. Kerry was coming, now! For some reason, this little guy was determined to leave the soothing womb that had comforted him, to a noisy, bright neonatal intensive care unit where the team of medical professionals worked intently to meet his multitude of immediate needs. The room was filled with everyone in "moon suits" and bright lights and intense fear. The whole delivery scene wasn't the typical anxious elation one normally expects. Once their son was delivered there were no cheers because they knew that statistically boys have a lower survival rate than girls. Even a girl had only a 10% survival rate at 25 weeks gestation. Even with all this skill and knowledge and technology, Kerry's survival was truly minute-by-minute. No hope was offered to these new parents.

After two days in critical condition, Deanna asked to hold her son. Kerry's dad, Eric, explained that Kerry was just too small. Deanna had to strain for a quick vision of his first born son immediately after delivery, and remembered him being incredibly small and red and his cries were almost inaudible. The little cry sounded similar to the cries of a newborn kitten. She described his tiny face as being only about the size of a small plum. She couldn't hold him, but she desperately wanted to get a good look at her son. That would have to wait. He was still in critical condition. His eyes were fused shut, and his arms were about the width of her index finger. His skin was bright red and any touch tore it. His body vibrated as the oscillator pushed air in and out of his body. All this didn't hinder Deanna's instant and unconditional love for her new son, but along with that love was more fear than she ever imagined.

Eric and Deanna quickly learned to celebrate important milestones. These aren't the usual milestones that families celebrate. These were things most of us take for granted like breathing on one's own, not having to fight to stay alive, surviving to see one more shift change of the nursing staff. These milestones were numbered by days. One such milestone was when Kerry made it to day number four. Deanna was able to greet her newborn son with a kiss for the first time.

When Kerry precariously made it to a month old, Deanna was able to hold him for the first time. This was bittersweet because he was at his sickest point, with sepsis. But he made it through that and on to three months old. That was when he could be breast-fed for the first time.

When Kerry persevered to 4 ½ months old, he finally got to go home. After agonizing over the death of many other premature babies while at the NICU, this homecoming was more precious than ever. They rejoiced over being able to take their baby home and live as a family.

This delicate little boy has survived jaundice, bilateral brain bleeds - grade 2 with brain damage, sepsis, pneumonia, retinopathy of prematurity, laser surgery on his eyes, hernia surgeries, broncho pulmonary dysplasia, severe epilepsy, reflux, exploratory surgery for suspected NEC, multiple transfusions, osteopenia, dependence to opiates for pain, muscle immaturity and extreme tightness, he was on oxygen until 3 years old, has been diagnosed with developmental delays in all areas, hypersensitivity to noises, touch, taste, and movements, and asthma. Keep in mind all these maladies have afflicted a child only six years old. But you should see him!

He reminds me of the phrase, "You must have been a beautiful baby, cause baby, look at you now!"

When Kerry was assigned to my room, our Intermediate Unit (IU) alerted me of all his special needs. They weren't sure this child would even function in a "normal" classroom, but they wanted to try. Since they predicted he would disrupt our environment, the recommendation was for him to start attending only three days a week. I was warned that he didn't share well, took temper tantrums, hit others, and threw toys. He was identified with a speech and language delay, which made it difficult to understand his needs. It wasn't certain how his health would hold out; so a nurse might accompany him. This is just what every preschool teacher wants to hear about an upcoming student. I was apprehensive, to say the least.

Then this dear, sweet child entered my room. I fell in love with him in about two minutes flat. His unique style of expressing himself made him even more endearing. I would ask him to do something, and he'd respond, "Awkay," in a drawn out voice that looked like it took genuine effort to move his mouth to form the word. But he did it, and it was so sweet. After two weeks in our class, all my preconceived notions about this child had subsided. I couldn't see any reason to continue Kerry's attendance on a limited basis; so I called the I U and suggested we let him attend daily. The IU coordinators and the parents were thrilled.

Our staff learned and appreciated many things about Kerry. First we were delighted to discover that Kerry has a great sense of humor. He likes to tease and be teased. His occupational therapist's name was Mrs. Rosenberger, and he called her "Mrs. Hamburger." Then we had the honor of seeing Kerry's unconditional love for animals when a visitor brought two dogs to school to play one day. Kerry wouldn't stop hugging them. After that, Kerry became the official hugger in our room, and he made sure everyone received a hug.

I can't explain how a tiny little body could radiate so much joy but Kerry could do it. When he laughed, it filled the room. He would scrunch up his cute little nose which would make his glasses slide up past his eyebrows and make a snorting sound as he cocked his head to one side. The last day of classes before Christmas break he arrived at school wearing a red Rudolf nose that lit up and antlers on his head. It was so-o incredibly adorable and he knew it!

The joy Kerry radiated was so apparent that we decided to let him role model his joy so as to positively influence other students behavior. This assignment made him grow inches taller. He liked this role and didn't take it lightly. Kerry's unconditional joy was spread to staff when he would ask them to draw the red Power Ranger. None of us were even close to drawing with the ability his mother possessed, but he wasn't critical. He never asked for much. Outsiders felt his joy, too. When visitors came to our classroom, they immediately singled out Kerry and asked the name of this dear, sweet, gentle, kind, cute little fellow. I was very proud to answer, "That's our Kerry!" Everyone got to know Kerry in that way, and not as the child who was identified with multiple disabilities and needs.

We had a tendency to want to protect Kerry because he appeared to be so fragile; but he wanted to play rough and tough like some of the other children. When he would get knocked down, we'd go running but he was already picking himself up, reassuring us that, "I aw right!" Part of the reason we felt we had to protect him came from our predisposed perception of his limitations due to his label. But the labels that preceded Kerry weren't accurate in a non-clinical way. He put all stereotypes regarding his disabilities quickly to rest. His label should have been, "Be careful! This child is very easy to fall in love with."

I remember another child who exceeded the limitations her label implied. She had been assigned a special need aide only because she had a label; typically Down's kids need some extra one-on-one instruction and assistance. But not Lindsey. She didn't need this extra supervision nor did she want it. She wanted to be independent like all the other kids. She was a sweetheart of a child and didn't cause any disruption or impede the learning of any other student in our class. She did just fine on her own. Just because she had a label, many people expected certain things from her, including minimal accomplishments.

What's frustrating is when a child needs the extra support, but no assistance can be obtained because a "label" hasn't been assigned. The process to diagnose a child with special needs, which are evident through problematic behavior, is long and often without resolve. There have been many times I have begged for extra support for a child with extreme behavioral problems but have been told to just "deal with it" because it is difficult to determine needs based on behavior. A child with an official medical diagnosis is considered more needy. Actually I have found, often times, that the kids with identified needs are the least needy in a school setting.

Forget labels when working with kids. That child is more than the stereotyped label with which they have been branded. Who benefits from these labels? Is it the child? Sometimes a label becomes an excuse for ill-behavior. Sometimes it is perceived that if a child has a label, they can't be held accountable for their actions. There are hundreds of labels that can be bestowed on a child. This can be dangerous because children are treated differently when they have a fancy label. "I must not be labeled. I have a right to be recognized as the person I am. Any true understanding of who I am will include knowledge of disability, but I must never be identified as disability label." This was adapted from a book titled, <u>The Beliefs, Values, and Principles of Self-advocacy </u>by the International league of Society for Persons with Mental Handicaps. 1994.

When our students are ready to move on, we assist with their transition to kindergarten. I am always careful to describe the child, not the label with which the child has been branded. I speak mostly of the child's strengths, not his impairments, the child's character, his virtues, his likes and dislikes. Advocating Change Together, a grassroots disability rights organization run by and for people with disabilities, recently published in the Self-Advocacy Resource Network Memo that, *"Stereotypes hurt people by making them feel less valued by society. People who are labeled often have trouble having their voice heard, because society does not think they have anything valuable to say. People with disabilities are one group that is often hurt by stereotyping. Labels like 'retarded,' 'handicapped,' and 'crippled' can keep these people trapped in a box. It can be hard for others in society to see who people with disabilities really are. Rather, others tend to only see the 'disability,' the wheelchair, or other assistive devices. They don't see the person at all. Labels like these are not only bad for the people being labeled; they are also bad for society. Why? Because as people feel de-valued, their gifts and talents are ignored, and when their gifts are not used to make the world a better place to live, society loses out."*

Marva Collins, a nationally known educator who concentrates on teaching as well as on creating and implementing, states, "Students do not need to be labeled or measured by more than they are. They don't need more federal funds, grants, and gimmicks. What they need from us is common sense, dedication, and bright, energetic teachers who believe that all children are achievers and who take personally the failure of any one child."

Iyanla Vanzant writes in her book, <u>One Day My Soul Just Opened Up,</u> in the chapter, Honor the Divine with Creativity: *"Fear is born of a lack of understanding, the need to control, and, more important, the absence of love. Christians can't love the Muslims. Muslims can't love the Jews. It's actually not true that they can't love each other, it's just real hard to move beyond the labels. Boy! Have we created some angry labels! Punk! Nigger! Bitch! Fag! Kike! Dyke! Spic! Pig! Fatty! Skinny! You tag one of these labels on somebody and they are sure to get mad at you. If you say it aloud, you should probably be afraid. And you know what? You don't even have to say what you are thinking out loud. If you think it hard enough, the object to which your thoughts are directed may hate you or be afraid of you and not* be able to explain why. *In some cases, people can actually feel what you think about them. That's just how powerful we are."*

I've heard the medical community is also becoming aware of viewing patients as individuals instead of labeling them as an illness. It is no longer acceptable to refer to Mrs. Johnson as, "the abscess in four." That tells you nothing about the person in room four. If medical personnel do not like to deal with abscesses, they are going to walk into that room with preconceived notions of that patient and the problem. That patient has more needs than that abscess. That patient still wants to be treated for who he is and not any different from the abrasion in room two.

When a child is assigned to my room with a label, he doesn't want to be treated any differently. One reason to which I attribute my success with autistic students is that I don't have any lesser expectations of them than other students. I require them to meet and try to exceed to their highest level of development, just like all the other kids. I hope kids don't know they are labeled, "Different." Kerry certainly never thought himself to be different. He is definitely special (in a positive way), but not different. He is just like everyone else in that he just wants to be loved for who he is.

Chapter Twelve

Braydon

Braydon taught me .... I must let go of perceived failures and celebrate successes.

Braydon was a dear, sweet boy with autism. His parents were wonderful. Every child should be so lucky as to have parents as involved and concerned as Braydon's. They wanted the best for Braydon. And I feel as though I didn't provide them with that. I feel I was a disappointment to them and to myself. Although I had delighted in great successes with autistic kids in the past, this year was different.

This year was the most challenging and demanding class of my career. I had a class size of twenty when eighteen is the norm. I had a severe behavior problem child and my aide was frequently absent due to illness. Our agency developed a new assessment tool, which required much observation and note taking during class time with students.

Braydon had a Therapeutic Staff Support (T.S.S), which means Braydon had an aide just for him. This aide was to help Braydon function normally in a mainstreamed classroom. When I gave a direction, the aide helped Braydon comply, as any other "normal" child would do on his own. That's how, ideally, it's supposed to work. And that is how it had effectively worked in past situations involving a T.S.S. in my classroom. Well, I guess I was speaking a foreign language to this aide because when I directed her to try a behavior plan with Braydon, she would follow-through, maybe once, and then never implement the plan again. I would model how I wanted a situation handled; again, poor follow-through. Since a T.S.S. is contracted through a different agency it is a touchy situation when there is dissatisfaction with one's performance. Also, it is the parent's right to request a different worker, not mine, but whose responsibility is it to squeal on the worker's poor performance? A lot of red tape and a lot of politics were in play here. To make things worse, a behavior specialist, employed by the same agency, as the T.S.S., was frequently absent from her job that year. The behavior specialist's job is to observe a child in the classroom and develop a behavior plan for the T.S.S. and, when possible, the teacher to follow. In Braydon's case, the behaviorist didn't visit my classroom until February, and that was only after I pressed for it. I had to remind that agency that Braydon's education plan required the services provided by the behaviorist. Braydon was falling through the cracks and I was frustrated with the entire situation.

Then to make things worse, the T.S.S., who must have realized I was at the end of my rope with her, went behind my back, to the already overwhelmed mom, and reported that she was the only one who truly cared about Braydon, and added some other manipulating comments. The poor mom didn't know what to think. It was all very unfair and understandably confusing to her.

Meanwhile, in my classroom, the behavior problem child required one-on-one assistance. That is where I had to be to ensure the safety of all the students. We also had to handle the occasional outburst from other students and the quiet needs of the rest. Once again Braydon was getting lost through the cracks, both in my overwhelming classroom and the agencies involved.

After the mom sorted it all out she decided to ask for a new T.S.S. The new aide assigned to him understood my direction and followed through! We were thrilled. O.K. We're cooking now! Braydon can finally get the individual direction he needs and we can keep working on the remainder of the class. Things were going great - then she quit. She took a job with another agency. What a disappointment! Again Braydon was falling victim to unfortunate circumstances.

I was hopeful that the replacement would be as effective as the one who just quit, but no such luck. The next T.S.S. was just a big kid. He was more interested in playing with our toys than instructing Braydon. I often had to remind him to face Braydon and direct him to assemble a puzzle even though I was quite impressed that the T.S.S. could assemble our 11 piece puzzles all by himself! On the playground we had to keep a very watchful eye on Braydon along with 19 others because the T.S.S. would daydream while sitting on a bench and Braydon would begin to wander away until my aide or I would redirect him. I repeatedly explained to the

T.S.S. about the safety issue at hand here but it was apparent he wanted to do as little as possible for his paycheck The T.S.S. could have been a good buddy to Braydon but that's not what he needed. Braydon had plenty of buddies. He needed a mature, responsible, caring adult to pilot him through normal everyday activities. I didn't want to be unprofessional, but I wanted to report the inadequacies of this guy, too. At that point I knew the parents were totally frustrated with the whole expectation-shattering experience, and I was totally frustrated with the situation and the whole year. I questioned, "Would it help anyone at his stage to point out more downfalls?" I decided it wouldn't. I just kept my frustrations to myself and accepted defeat. I realized one can only do so much. I didn't know why fate had handed me this brick wall and why Braydon had to be the cement between the bricks but I had little control over the circumstances. There is no justification for not meeting Braydon's needs but I know I honestly did the best I could. I was still disappointed in myself and the entire situation. I had to force myself to remember past successes. I realized one disappointing outcome doesn't negate all the positive impacts I've had on the lives of many other children.

As I reflect at the end of a school year, I am mindful to celebrate and contemplate what did work, as well as what didn't. I recently heard another teacher speak about a young child in her room. She said, "I don't have time to teach him. He's learning daily just by being here." What a cop-out! Although I couldn't believe those words and that attitude came out of any professional in the teaching field; I recognized she was burned out and her need for a break.

This situation made me know what she felt like. I even questioned whether I was getting too old for this job or not. That's when I started the catharsis of writing this book. The sad reality is that we can't always provide what each individual child needs. It's nobody's fault, just an unfortunate fact. It falls under the category of "Life isn't fair!" But I do what I can do. The children move on and I need to also. I have learned that I will do everything I can to not let another child slip through the cracks but reality is, another one probably will. There is a national slogan right now, "No child left behind." It's a great philosophy and goal because it takes a team. One person can't do it alone. A more fitting slogan is, "It takes a village" because we all need to work together to meet the needs of each and every child. I am striving to do my part. That's all I can do.

Chapter Thirteen

Anna

Anna taught me – some parents just don't get it.

Thank goodness Anna was an only child and I don't say that because she born with the degenerative, fatal disease of cystic fibrosis, which was worsened by her 100 pound body at the age of four. This extra weight made it even harder for her to breathe, which meant that on her good days, she needed breathing treatments at least two times. The average life span for someone afflicted with this is only 30 years. I started by saying, "thank goodness," because Anna's mom's priorities were not focused on maximizing Anna's potential. Mom's priorities where on keeping an immaculate house rather than letting Anna enjoy finger painting. She apparently thought it was more important to smoke cigarettes than for Anna to breathe clean air. She berated Anna for her extra needs.

It just didn't make sense to me. There are so many people out there who would give anything for a healthy child and so many people who would do anything for their sick child. Anna didn't ask for any of the extra care she required. She just wanted loving, selfless, nurturing parents to care for her in a manner that would facilitate the healthiest, most fulfilling life she could possibly have. She didn't intend to be an extra burden. She just wanted to be cared for unconditionally.

One of a child's greatest needs is to feel unconditional love and acceptance by at least one person. In our performance-based society, some children never experience this. Our children are weighed, measured, tested, and compared from the day they are born and, in some cases, never feel valued for the unique person they are. Our society places more value on performance than on person hood. We educators must make sure that at least one person tells that child, "I think you are special, just because you're you." It's easy to forget children need to hear and feel that because they give unconditional love. That is one of the amazing things about children. They love you anyway. They love you if you punish them, they love you when you're happy, mad, sad; on good days and bad, even when they are mad at you. They love you anyway. This innate survival instinct to love is something that I see too many parents take advantage of and take for granted. Fortunately, not all parents though.

I used to provide respite care for a little girl who had cerebral palsy. She had never been capable of feeding herself or dressing herself or using a toilet, talking or walking. But she was one of the luckiest little girls I have known, because her parents loved her completely. They cared for her as though she were a queen. How lucky indeed.

Another little girl I cared for had such severe brain damage that her brain couldn't even send the message to signal her to cough. She could, literally, drown in her own saliva. She had severe seizures throughout each day and night. She was fed with an n-g tube initially, then through a stomach tube. She needed constant, round-the-clock care. Her parents were diligent and caring. When her short life ended, her mom said, "If she just could have smiled at me once, it would have made it all okay." That's all that mom asked in return for all her selfless caring for her child. Just one little smile. She never got it but she never stopped putting the needs of her daughter above her own. That mom "got it!" Unfortunately, there are plenty who don't, though.

I worked with a child who had been placed in foster care. My co-workers and I could not understand why this foster mom took on the responsibility of being a parent to this beautiful little girl. Over the first month of placement in this foster home, we watched this happy-go-lucky precious little girl, turn inward and look fearful of the world. Coming to school was her greatest joy until it was time to board the bus and depart for home. Big, sorrowful, fearful tears would wail out of her. She would beg each member of our staff to let her go home with them. Knowing that this indicated big problems, I discussed with a co-worker the gravity of this child's reaction. I voiced that I know children who come from homes of an alcoholic, abusive parent and that child still wants to go home. So we began reporting to the foster agency. Eventually, this little girl was placed in a home as beautiful as she is. To me, her first foster mom had NO excuse. It's not like she had an unplanned pregnancy and was trying to accept the responsibilities nature thrust upon her. She chose to take this child. Doesn't she see what she is doing to this child? Is she in denial, is she sadistic, or narcissistic? All I know is it isn't fair to this innocent child who is reliant, and not by choice, on this woman who took on the all-important role of mom only to crush the very spirit of a precious little child

Other indications that parents don't get it are visible everyday. I still see children riding in the front sear of the car unrestrained. I still see children riding bicycles and 4-wheelers without helmets. I still see children unsupervised in the mall. I still see children eating entirely too much sugar and fat products just because it's easy. I still see children leading sedentary lives. I still see parents smoking around their asthmatic child. I still see children watching adult movies. I still hear about children being offered alcoholic beverages. I've seen parents routinely fill an infant's baby bottle with soda pop. I've heard children spoken to like the scripts of XXX-rated movies. I still see children being punished for developmentally appropriate behavior. I still see children being taught hate and prejudice. Yes, that is taught; it is not something we are born with. I still see children who don't feel loved, appreciated, and wanted. I still hear about children who have been neglected. I still see children being emotionally scarred for life. I still see children who have been beaten. I see pregnant mothers complain about their other children.

Don't they get it? Don't they get that having children is an honor and a privilege, not a right. Don't they understand children have a right to be treated, at least, as well as someone's beloved pets are treated? Don't they understand parenting is a 24/7 job? Don't they realize that parenting is extremely difficult, not just a fantasy of holding a cute little, smiling baby? Raising children isn't easy, but creating anything worthwhile isn't easy, and children are worth every ounce of energy they can be given.

Another child showed me that some parents just don't "get" that children's well-being should come first. Isaiah has four siblings, one of which is his twin, which means his dad had to be out of jail long enough to procreate three times. This child told stories about visiting dad in the jail and having Easter at the jail and yelling to his dad through the window at the jail. This was common conversation and a "normal" way of life for this young child. He would brag about his dad beating up the neighbor or getting drunk or "taking" things that belonged to someone else. He has no idea that his dad's actions are considered by most of society as derelict. In his world, every kid visits their dad in jail because when he'd go for visitation day, other kids would be visiting their imprisoned parent, too. I spoke with the warden of our local jail. She said it is very common for the jail to be inhabited with generations of a family. It is just what they do. It is their way of life. It becomes a rite of passage to have done jail time. It is a challenge to see how many crimes can be committed before the perpetrator is caught. Modeling this way of life can't be conducive to a child's well-being.

A friend of mine got a cruel case of parents who just don't get it, when her six year old son decided to try wrestling. She witnessed a parent yelling obscenities at his son. She saw parents publicly humiliate and demean their sons. She saw a mom actually shake her son because he hadn't pinned his opponent. Then this mom threw her son at the dad who proceeded to head-butt him.

What is with these overly ambitious sports parents who aren't just proud their child is out there giving it his/her all? Their child has to be the "best" and win all the time or they just aren't good enough. It's great to want your child to succeed but they need your unconditional support to enable them to feel safe, secure and confident enough to do that.

At another wrestling match, a little boy who was putting all his 50 pounds of weight and muscle into the match, was overcome with the need to relieve some pressure and he passed gas. I've never been out there on the mat, but I'm sure that happens, unintentionally, quite frequently. Instead of making this little boy feel it was normal and okay, the coach called him, "Fart Boy," and encouraged six other little wrestlers to call him that, too. This embarrassed little boy held back tears until he made his way to his mom in the bleachers. Then the tears started to fall. A rough, tough dad of another boy who witnessed this said loudly enough for the dispirited little boy and his mom to hear, "Pussy." He added, "You're raising a Pussy Boy!" Can you imagine? I must be very naive, because I can't imagine thinking or saying that to anyone, anywhere. I respect that everyone has the right to his/her own opinion, but expressing it at the expense of hurting someone else, especially a child, is just wrong!

I remember being in a situation where I witnessed a scene that my sheltered upbringing had not prepared me for. A little girl, about five years old, had just crawled out of bed and sleepily descended the stairs. Her mother gave her a good morning greeting of, "Hey! You little bitch-whore! You get the Hell back upstairs!" The little girl stopped dead in her tracks. Just then the mom began laughing (I guess it was just a term of endearment! Yeah, right.) She told her daughter to come on downstairs. The little girls' reaction made it clear that this has happened before and when it happens, she has to wait to see if Mommy is serious that day, or just kidding.

A friend told me she witnessed the arrival of a family to a sporting practice. Upon noticing this mother was toting only two children when she usually had three in tow, she inquired as to the whereabouts of the third child. The mother said she must have left one of her children in her van. She leisurely walked back to her van and was surprised to see her four-year-old boy was not in there after-all. They looked around and discovered this scared little boy hiding under the front of the van. He had been sleeping when the other two children got out and when he awoke, alone, was frightened and got out of the van to find his mom. When he couldn't find her, he hid like a lost little rabbit under the van. Instead of this mom sensing her son's emotion and why he did what he did, she grabbed him out from under the van and began to spank him violently and yell at him for what he had supposedly done wrong. What this mom apparently didn't get is that he had done nothing wrong. I'm sure he needed reassured that Mommy was sorry for leaving him behind and would try her best to never be so preoccupied as to do that again. Instead, I'm sure he felt as though he got publicly humiliated. Poor little guy! The public humiliation is nothing compared to the feelings of confusion and abandonment and worthlessness that imbedded itself in a portion of his personality. Neale Donald Walsch, author of <u>Conversations With God</u> writes, "It only takes a few seconds to open profound wounds in those we love and it can take many years to heal them."

Unfortunately similar damaging incidences happen all too regularly. I was shocked to find out that child protection laws came into action in this country after animal abuse laws. Don't get me wrong, I am ALL for the humane and decent treatment of animals, but it's amazing to me that children didn't come first. Just a few instances of why we need child protection agencies, that I am painfully aware of, are recounted next.

A little six year old boy frequently rode the big rig with his dad. One day, they were stopped for a traffic violation. The little boy boldly said to the policeman, "Why don't you suck my dick!" The dad thought it was funny. He even showed pride when re-telling the story.

Another dad threatened to "beat his little girl" because she jumped up on his lap and innocently landed on his private parts with her knee.

I've heard of a girl, about five years old, telling her teacher that the only thing she had to eat over the weekend was cereal from the box she keeps hidden under her bed.

I've heard from a colleague that she witnessed an 18 month old being beaten in a grocery store after she cried for some food. Get it! She was repeatedly spanked for being hungry in a place so overwhelming stimulating that all of us have a difficult time quelling the urge to pig-out on everything in sight.

One of my sisters is a teacher in a secondary school. She tells about a parent who endlessly contacted the school on her child's behalf to complain that her son wasn't given one point higher on a paper which caused his grade to be a whole grade lower. This parent failed to mention that she hadn't held him accountable for a homework assignment which was worth 50 points. If he had just turned that in, the one point difference wouldn't have affected his total grade at all.

I still remember thinking "how ridiculous" when an old neighbor of mine was fighting with the authorities from her son's school because her son had been caught smoking on school grounds. She insisted that she allows her 16 year old son to smoke, so the school had no right to punish him for smoking. What kind of message is that sending to the child? Not the message that laws are to be obeyed, that's for sure.

My sister has been repeatedly frustrated by parents standing-up for their child in all the wrong ways. This sends very damaging messages to the child. First, do what you want and Mommy or Daddy will get you out of it. Then, don't worry about suffering consequences for the choices you make. And, when in trouble, just get loud and boisterous. And on and on and on. You get the picture.

When dealing with children, we need to be concerned with what the long-term effect is going to be. It seems as though parents want to have perfect children without being responsible parents. Perfect people do not exist but perfect intention is all we need to strive for because it can negate all the mistakes we make along the way. Nobody plans to have 'bad kids.' Parents usually think those kind of kids always belong to someone else. So I can do whatever I want and not worry because my kids will turn out all right. If the kids don't, it's someone else's fault. It's the school's fault, or the neighbor's or the coach's or the grandparent's or the day care or the babysitter's.........or........or......or.

I get extremely frustrated when I hear, "That kid is messed up because her parents divorced." Bull crap! The act of divorce doesn't mess up kids. If this were true, then every child from a divorced family would be a mess, and I can cite many well-balanced adults who came from divorced parents. It would also mean that every child from a couple that stayed together is absolutely well-adjusted and "normal." Not true either. The determining factor is how the parents behave before, during and after a divorce. Too many parents use their children as leverage to try to get and then keep a partner, then to hurt the partner when it doesn't work out. This kind of behavior is what messes up kids. They are used not taken care of. They are wrongly thrown in the middle of adult issues. Issues that are too advanced for their young minds to comprehend. Whether the parents reside in the same home or not, kids need to know they are loved and cared for and are special to both parents. I've seen too many children scarred because the parents "stayed together for the kids." How is that going to teach the children how to treat his or her mate when they grow up? How are they going to learn to make the tough decisions in life? How are they going to learn that you don't have to please everyone around you all the time? How are they going to learn self-respect and self-preservation? How can they be happy when they are being raised by unfulfilled, unhappy parents? A study by E. Mavis Hetherington and John Kelly concludes that 75% of children with divorced parents end up as happy and well adjusted as their counterparts with intact families. In a study of more than 1400 families, it was found that, "The other 20% developed some kind of psychological, emotional, or academic problems, compared to 10% of the non-divorced group." A colleague of mine has hit the nail on the head with his observation of the change in students over the past 15-20 years. He stated that "parents divorcing is not the cause of children's problems. It's the time. The problem is the amount of time a parent gives to her child. Parents aren't giving their children enough of their time these days."

A friend of mine recently went through a divorce. He has done an honorable job of making sure the needs of his three children still and always will come first. But he made an interesting point. He explained that his parents never divorced but feels he is screwed-up anyhow. Mostly because his dad never told him he loved him or was proud of him or any of those important, crucial messages we all need to feel and hear from our parents. He feels he's a better parent now that he is divorced because he is more fulfilled in other areas of his life so he has more to give. When I was struggling with marital strife, I was so consumed and overwhelmed that I felt I couldn't even be a good teacher, let alone a good parent. So I totally related and understood and concurred. Lisa Whaley, author of Reclaiming My Soul From the Lost and Found, talked about her husband leaving her and her daughters. She stated, "He just couldn't help Kristin or me because he was lost in grief, anger, and resentment." She knew they needed a "time-out" because "our relationship had become unhealthy for our kids and for us." Very wise perspective. Some couple would stay together, thinking it is for the sake of the children, when in reality staying together is counter-productive to healthy children. The whole family goes down then. Save yourself and you will be saving your children from the inevitable downward spiral as well. When my god children were told their parents were planning to divorce, Hannah asked, "Can't you fix it?" Her father answered very wisely, "This is how to fix it." Vince Lombardi, one of footballs most accomplished coaches, once said, "Just because you're doing something wrong, doing it more intensely isn't going to help."

Another friend explains that she feels she has issues because her parents didn't divorce. She said their continued union taught her to stay no matter what; to stuff her own feelings; that she didn't have a right to her own feelings; not to trust her own mind; and that she has to please everyone around her. She feels that if her mom would have left her dad when she was young, it would have modeled for her that to trust your instincts; to be strong; to be confident; to not tolerate being treated anything less than spectacularly; and to have healthy self-respect and independence. That would have saved her from many challenging struggles she has faced in her adult life. Dr. Phil, psychologist and author, frequently states, "Children would rather come from a broken home than live in a broken home." If children live in a broken home, they will learn a broken way of life.

A beautiful poem came to me "author Unknown" and is titled "Children Live What They Learn.

If a child lives with criticism, he learns to condemn.
If a child lives with hostility, he learns to fight.
If a child lives with ridicule, he learns to be shy.
If a child lives with shame, he learns to feel guilty.
If a child lives with tolerance, he learns to be patience.
If a child lives with encouragement, he learns confidence.
If a child lives with praise, he learns to appreciate.
If a child lives with fairness, he learns justice.
If a child lives with security, he learns to have faith.
If a child lives with approval, he learns to like himself.
If a child lives with acceptance and friendship, he learns to find love in the world."

I add to that: If a child lives violence, they learn violence. If a child lives crime, they commit crimes. If a child lives love, they learn love. If a child lives promiscuity, they learn promiscuity. If a child lives prejudice, they learn prejudice. If a child lives with good manners, they learn good manners. If a child lives in filth, they learn to live in filth. If a child lives with overindulgence, they learn overindulgence. If a child lives right and wrong, they learn right and wrong. If the child lives with spankings, they learn to hit. It sounds too simple but it really is just that simple.

It surprises me that some parents become angry with still another food stained shirt when they've never used napkins in their home. Or the parents who have filed for bankruptcy but can't understand why their child can't budget money and demands everything right now.

This chapter is not meant to slander any parents. We all make errors in good judgment. I don't mean for it to sound judgmental. It's just hard for me to believe that these examples represent everyday reality to thousands of innocent children in America who just want to be loved and accepted and appreciated, but are living a life which makes them learn the opposite.

Bruce Lipton, cellular biologist, author and acclaimed speaker said, "The chemistry of the developing fetus is affected by the chemistry of the mother. What the mother experiences, the child also experiences. This sends important information to the cells of the developing fetus, preparing it for the inevitable emergence into the world. Your experiences from the moment of conception are creating memories, receptors, and programmed responses. It is this kind of preconditioning that helps ensure survival of the baby as it enters its new world outside the womb. It is nature's way of educating the child to his or her environment before having to deal with it directly, thereby increasing the odds for the survival of the child." Just because children have been pre-wired to deal with the environment into which they are born, doesn't mean they should have to live in substandard conditons. No one should be used to or get used to disrespectful parenting or being unhappy and unfulfilled. The Dalai Lama, author of <u>The Spontaneous Fulfillment of Desire,</u> states, "The purpose of our lives is to be happy." Happy children don't come from unhappy parents. And happy adults rarely come from parents who had been unhappy.

Actions really do speak louder than words. We must teach by example. Kids don't raise themselves. Everything that happens around them imprints who they are and who they will become. Their environment sends a message to them as to how one behaves and chooses to handle life's situations. It fossilizes in their characters.

To the parents that 'get it' - thank you from me and all of society. To those who don't, please open your eyes and see what you are teaching your child. I doubt it's what you expected.

If you get nothing else, please get this - parent your children responsibly with insight, foresight, patience and nurturing love. Be their hero. Be the one she looks up to and is proud of. Get this and they'll grow into the kind of people you can look up to and be proud of. Get this and you'll have it all.

Chapter Fourteen

Shawnee

Shawnee taught me – Let your children be children.

Shawnee was the only child of a very flamboyant mother. This mother loved Halloween and was proud of having what it takes to portray an unbelievably convincing witch. It was actually so real, it was unnerving. Especially after she revealed to me that she practiced magic and even offered to share some "spells" with me. I'm pretty open-minded but this concerned me to the point that I darn well made sure I stayed on the good side of her!

If that was as far as this mom's unconventional views went I wouldn't have questioned it but she also thought it was acceptable that her daughter was four going on seventeen! She encouraged Shawnee to flirt with boys and men. She teased Shawnee about having a "boyfriend" when she saw Shawnee talking or playing with a boy in the class. She would ask if she was going to "kiss her new boyfriend" more extremely than what most people consider normal teasing.

One day my husband visited at school. Shawnee immediately took an interest in him and would not leave his side, typical behavior for her with any male visitor. I couldn't believe it as I watched her bat her eye lashes at him and alluringly draw circles on his thighs with her index finger. I alerted my unaware husband to promote her to interact appropriately with him. Once he was made aware that her actions were not typical, innocent four-year-old overtures he tried to go to other parts of the room but Shawnee followed him like a shadow. At lunchtime, guess who sat beside him? Yep,

Shawnee positioned herself strategically beside him and rested her head on his arm. As much as she tried to emulate adult-like innuendoes, the little girl in her came out when she looked adoringly at him and said, in her most seductive voice (and she did try to speak in a seductive voice!) "I just put a boogie on your leg!" My husband laughs until he cries to this day about that. What we don't laugh about is that we think she meant that offering as sexy. That part is not funny. That child is being set up for some serious consequences that she isn't mature enough to handle, I'm afraid.

I am horrified at stories of parents encouraging their daughters to form a bond with every fly-by-night boyfriend/girlfriend they bring into the house. I am appalled at stories of little 12 year olds being encouraged by their parents to portray themselves seductively on websites. What are they thinking? What is this teaching those children? Do they honestly not realize the huge risk at which they are putting their babies? I have a hard time believing that they could think this is okay and is not harming their child emotionally, let alone the potential for physical danger from this kind of adult advertisement. The world can be pretty ugly. Parents should protect their children from it not let their children contribute to that side of it. A friend of mine had to disappoint her nine year old daughter when she refused to let her leave the house with her jeans tugged way low so she could show off her navel. The daughter thought it is was cool. The mom knew the dangers of this kind of advertising and did what a responsible parent has to do. It isn't easy, but it is necessary.

For children to have healthy self-esteem, they need to feel good about who they are, not what they look like or who thinks they are pretty or who they can attract. In the day when our court system has to struggle with juvenile offenders as young as six, it is not the time to promote growing up too quickly. Children grow up quickly enough and have to deal with adult issues all their adult life.

A child's only stress should be if they are going to be able to play on the playground that day or not; or if she can make it through a meal without spilling her drink; or if Daddy packed an orange instead of a banana in their lunch; or hoping they get through the day with dry undies.

Let them have the innocence of youth. You know, when little girls think a boyfriend is just a little playmate who happens to stand up to pee. Or at a little bit older stage in life, when a girl thinks boys are "yuccky." The wonderful magic of innocence when one still believes in Santa Claus; the Easter Bunny; the tooth fairy and Mickey Mouse. The innocence that works in our favor like when kids think we are brilliant because we can tell time or know where the ocean is or all the words to a song. The earnest innocence when they look at you in total awe and ask, "How do you know that?" The innocence that lets you harmlessly fool children by pretending to find a quarter from behind their little ear or pretend the dog really is talking to you.

I was able to spend time in Switzerland and was pleasantly surprised to discover that the children there are still able to delight in the innocence of youth. I saw children running naked through a sprinkler system in the middle of the capital, Bern. No one thought anything bad or perverted about this. Children can and do still enjoy doing this. Children are able to enjoy playing outside without being directly supervised. Children can roam the toy section of a store while the parent shops in another part of the store. Children, as young as five, are peaceful as they independently walk to school without fear of a stranger grabbing them.

The Swiss children reminded me of how the world was when I grew up. My parents could let me and my siblings leave the house, without worry, in the morning and not come home until dark. They just knew we were running around the neighborhood and we were okay. We could go Trick-or-Treating without supervision and without having our candy inspected before ingesting. This and many more freedoms are a lost luxury these days. Now even when a child is playing within the confines of ones own fenced-in yard, their parents need to keep vigil. How do you strike a balance between allowing children enough autonomy to develop a sense of competence and confidence and still keep them safe? It's a struggle, especially to do it without unnecessarily frightening children. I remember when parents didn't have to cringe when they turned on the radio or television because they were afraid of inappropriate content. Now it is hard-pressed to find a song or a TV show without vulgarity or sexual or violent suggestions. L. Brent Bozell: founder and president of Parents Television Council states, "Protecting children from television, the Internet and video games: All three have programming and commercials that are produced for and marketed to children, but the material is designed to rob them of their innocence by flooding them with adult matter that they can't process and shouldn't have to confront." There is actually a popular song right now that teaches youth how to cut themselves. It explains how to do it, when to do it, where to do it. It conveys the message that one should do it when feeling pressure because the act of cutting will relieve the pressure and all their troubles will flow away with the blood. Can you imagine? How irresponsible of society to permit this kind of misguided influence on the airwaves.

It seems as though the innocent pranks we played when we were children are being taken to a whole new, disturbing level. If driving 70 mph was "daring," now kids dare to speed over 120 mph. If sneaking a smoke in the bathroom was rad, now kids take hits of heroin. If making out was being "grown-up," now having multiple sexual partners in one night before the age of 15 seems the norm.

The innocence of youth can never be replaced or regained. Let children enjoy this once-in-a-lifetime opportunity when they are young. I think we would all like to revisit the innocence of childhood. Sometimes we can feel the wonderment of childhood through our children. That's how it should be not the other way around. Children should not feel the corruption and stress of adulthood.

Our children should be blanketed with the age of innocence much the same way the fresh and clean fallen snow protects young plants. Then we can marvel at how they bloom in the Spring. If not protected, they die under the harsh, cold winter snow. They have the rest of their lives to be demoralized adults, let them be innocent children now.

Chapter Fifteen

Craig

Craig taught me......................money can't buy happiness.

Craig is the youngest of four children. Three of the four children have been in my class over the years. Each child has big, beautiful brown eyes and an abundance of sincere smiles. Some people may wonder what these children have to smile about.

When I first met the family, they lived in a small trailer that had holes in the floor and an old pot-belly cook stove in the 6 X 8 living room. Duct tape covered holes in the ceiling in an attempt to keep out inclement weather. Cleanliness was apparently not a necessity for them. The floor was littered with old food, clothes, toys and who-knows-what, to the extent that I have no idea what floor covering this dwelling contained. When I returned to enroll the third child, it appeared that nothing had been picked up from two years earlier, only added to.

During this child's school year, the family moved after child protective services declared the housing to be sub-standard. They returned about one year later and the six members of this family lived in a tiny camper, not much larger than the coach depicted in the story of Cinderella. They stated this was only temporary as they built a house. When I made the next home visit in the spring, they were living in their "new house." It was an 8 X 10 room without any windows. It was essentially a wooden box with clear plastic for a roof. When I returned in the fall, it was now an 8 X 20 structure. The only electric was provided through an extension cord from a neighboring house. The only water supply came from a garden hose, also tapped into the neighbor's house. But they proudly called it "home." The wooden structure withstood high winds from a hurricane but the plastic roof was blown off. They eventually put on a wooden roof then covered that with plastic. That's all they could afford. And yet, they smiled! Because within those four chip board walls, children were treated with unconditional love and respect. Wonderful morals, values and manners were taught. These children, who often wore clothes pulled out of a heap on the floor and continued to wear them, at times, for five days in a row; were some of the most delightful, pleasant, respectful, kind, and most considerate children you'd ever have the pleasure of meeting. They were comfortable around adults but independent enough to go play without much supervision. They always appreciated what they got and always genuinely said, please and thank you. They accepted being told "no," without pouting, whining or defiance, and without fear. They were always ready and willing to help in any way they could. They knew the difference between right and wrong and felt good about choosing the right way. They seemed to have a true understanding of, and appreciation and gratitude for life and living. Richard Carlson states in his book, <u>Stop Thinking Start Living</u>, the essence these children conveyed: "Gratitude is an attitude towards life that has nothing whatsoever to do with what you have or don't have. This is why you will often meet people who on the surface have little to be grateful for, but who feel a genuine sense of deep gratitude for the gift of life. These people aren't fooling themselves with their gratitude — they simply have a positive attitude. They look at what they have while most others focus on what they don't have." If you look at what's really important in life, this family had it all - the things that money can't buy, hurricanes can't blow away; the things that are irreplaceable.

A dear friend of mine, who is a doctor and father of two wonderful children, asks to be reminded frequently to not purchase all the toys his children ask for. He has equated being a good dad and successful business man with showering his children with their every whim and desire. Now he is seeing the affects of this unnecessary overindulgence. The children have conceptualized that if someone loves them, they will buy them something. The children do not appreciate what is purchased for them or the opportunities afforded them. The children have learned if they display a temper tantrum, their wishes will be fulfilled. And, the sad thing is, they still aren't happy. If this continues, will they ever be? Chances are, no. They are looking for their happiness from external sources. They are happy when they receive what they desired and then they desire something else. The pop song, "Calling All Angels" has a lyric, "In a world that what we want is only what we want until it's ours," is very accurate in this and many other cases.

Handing children everything they want is setting them up for a vicious cycle that ends in ungrateful, unhappy, unfulfilled adults. Ever know of an adult who gets a thrill from shopping for a new car or house? Two weeks after obtaining this item, he will start to become dissatisfied and start looking for the next purchase, so then he'll be satisfied, right? Wrong! This is the thinking of a shopaholic. This cycle is why we meet or hear about unhappy, unfulfilled wealthy people. Those of us with less money often think, "Man! If I just had her money!" Then what? You would still be you. You would still wake up the same and go to bed the same — with yourself. I'm not saying a person should give up goals, or shouldn't reap the financial benefits of her hard, diligent work, just don't count on it to make you happy; and don't set kids up to think having things is the ultimate goal.

I have more respect and admiration for the elderly lady who lives in a small, well-trodden trailer, who volunteers for hospice, feeds stay cats, takes meals to someone who is ill, remembers her friends and family on special occasions and buys Girl Scout cookies, than someone in a three piece suit that doesn't make time for his children, cuts his employees benefits, looks down on others with less, and worries about making another 20 grand this quarter. That kind of person may seem, on the outside, like he has it all, but if he looses his family, friends, integrity and self-respect in the process, what does he really have? Many events can take away material assets. Then what does he have? Just himself! And chances are, he doesn't like himself too well. Alicia Keys sings, "If I Ain't Got Nothing." A couple lines from that song state this philosophy: "Some people live for the fortune. Some people want diamond rings. Some people think a dozen roses and that's the only way to prove you love him. Some people think that the physical things define what's within and I bet that (those people) adore the superficial. Some just want everything. But everything means nothing." None of that means anything to a child. As Neale Donald Walsch wrote in Conversations With God, "A rich person is not the one who has the most, but one who needs the least."

I recently read a little story. I would love to give credit to the author, but it came to me "author unknown." It was titled "How Much Do You Make In An Hour?" A boy asked his father, "How much do you make in an hour?" The father got mad and answered roughly, "Don't bother me." He was tired and irritable after a tough day at work, but the boy insisted. "Please, how much do you make?" The father said in a bad tone of voice, "$8.00 dollars for now." Then the son asked, "Father, can you loan me four dollars?" The father said to him in a bad way, "I told you not to bother me, shut up and go to your room!" At bedtime the father was more calm and felt bad about the way he treated his son. He went upstairs to his son's room and asked,

"Are you asleep?" And he gave to the boy the four dollars that he asked for. The boy thanked his father, put his hand under his pillow, pulled out four crumpled dollars, and said, "I have $8.00 dollars, father could I buy one hour of your time?" There are too many children who would love to buy an hour of their parent's time. But the fact is money can't buy it - it's priceless. It needs to be given generously and freely.

Success comes in many forms. Craig and his family are a perfect example of that. Craig's parents have successfully instilled in their children an internal happiness, contentment and peace. Isn't that what we are all striving for? Material success often clouds all other aspects of success. That is why monks and great spiritual leaders go to a solitary, remote location, totally void of materialistic luxuries, to get in touch with what is really important. They discover who they really are without the power of money influencing them. When you strip away the material things, you see the naked truth of who you really are. I take the quote from Martin Luther King, "Judge not by the color of their skin but by the content of their character," and also think, "Judge not by their material possessions but by the content of their character."

Who you are travels with you, no matter where you go and no matter how much money you make. That is what others really value you for. This point was driven home to me after the tragedy of the terrorist attacks on 9-11. As loved ones spoke of the one they lost, they described the person; not what kind of car she drove, the value of her house, her income, or who's name was on the tag on her clothing. This just is not important. This is not what will be missed about that person. This is not who that person was and why that person was loved.

I always look at traffic jams as the great equalizer of life because no matter whether you drive a Lamborghini or a Pinto, you still sit bumper-to-bumper. There isn't anything you can do about it. You can't buy your way out of it. No matter what you drive, you are right in there with all the rest. And the value of your house is only apparent when you are there. When you go out in the world, it doesn't go with you. No one else knows. When you meet someone, they are meeting you, not your house. So it is important to care more for one's self and invest more internally than externally. This is what Craig's parents understood. This is what they taught me. Nathaniel Brandon, author and lecturer, said, "As children are raised to believe that who they are is what they have, a healthy sense of self is compromised." In other words, a healthy sense of self can't be bought.

It is easy to get caught up in this mindset that having more materialistically means having more happiness. Most of us are taught this from a very young age. Consider, for example, the story of Cinderella. It conveys that since she went from rags to riches she had it all. She is now happy and she and her Prince will "live happily ever after." Really? All the riches in the land doesn't guarantee happiness. It takes more than money to be a happily married couple. Children would rather have happy parents than wealthy parents.

A better lesson to convey to children is that happiness is always a thought away. Making lemonade from lemons is a valuable philosophy. It is a thought from which they can draw on the rest of their lives. Imagine the alternatives: "I can't make lemonade unless I have the best lemons from Florida and until I can have that, I have nothing!" Or worse yet, "Are you kidding? Me! Make lemonade? Never! I will pay someone else to make it for me!" Wow! A person with that attitude sure doesn't sound happy to me. They might be able to pay someone else to do work for them but I wonder how much better a person would feel if he would require more of himself and reap the benefits of getting his own hands dirty. It feels good knowing you did it yourself. This is why children say, "I can do it myself! I want to do it myself?" Sometimes this is aggravating as we wait for a child to do it himself, but think of what those couple extra minutes are creating in that child. That can't be bought.

I learned to be self-sufficient, and of that I am glad and proud. When I wanted to attend college, my father wasn't in agreement. He philosophized that since he attended school for only eight grades, and was able to become a successful businessman, no one should need more. He would say, "College makes a person an overeducated idiot!" He also thought that since I am a female, it would be a waste of time since I would end up staying home with children anyhow. And he had the hidden agenda of wanting me to take over running his business when he retired. This was not a desire of mine. I respect what my parents did in business, but it wasn't for me. I needed more rewards from my career than financial. So I pursued my own interests. I found ways to support myself through college.

At times, I must admit, I resented my dad for not funding my education. After all, he could have afforded to put me through Harvard. But what I didn't realize was that another education was simultaneously being provided through this endeavor. It taught me to be self-reliant, resourceful, appreciative, grateful, and gave me more self-esteem than anything in my life to that point. I can now say with pride, "I put myself through college!" and that has a value beyond any monetary price. I saw many students, while I was college, whose parents were funding their tuition and all other expenses. They even had a very nice car to drive. These students didn't seem to take their education seriously and didn't seem to appreciate their parents opening their bank accounts to them. Most of them just wanted more. They would actually complain because they had to settle for a Florida destination for spring break instead of Cancun. I looked forward to spring break because it gave me the opportunity to work more hours and make a little extra money. I was thrilled to make enough money to buy a new coat, which I really did need, not just want. I learned the value of a dollar. I learned to budget, save and wait. I learned it's an "eat what you kill world," and "waste not, want not." I could not have learned all this if my parents would have handed me everything my little heart desired. These lessons got me just as far in life, if not farther, than the lessons I learned sitting in a classroom. I don't resent my parents anymore for this lesson in the School of Hard Knocks. I thank them.

One of my favorite television shows is Andy Griffith. (Yes, my age is showing.) Most of the early shows have a moral lesson. One of my most memorable is when Opie breaks a window and must earn the money to buy a new window. In contrast, the show portrayed a spoiled young man who always had his wealthy dad buy his way out of trouble. Which method do you think will help a child grow into a responsible adult? Which kind of child do you want? The current program for which I am employed asks the parents, "What are your wishes and dreams for your child?" I also ask, "What do you want your child to grow up accomplishing and representing?" If asked those questions, would your only focus be on money? Would you want them to have a $500.000 a year job, or to be healthy, and be happy with whatever they have? It's daunting to remember that every decision you make concerning your child, goes into making that child an adult. Children don't stay children. We teach them so they can be responsible adults. Always ask, "What kind of adult do I want my child to be?" I doubt it's a spoiled brat who walks around with a warped sense of entitlement.

The reason I am telling all this is to impress upon you what is really important in the life of a child. Money is not important. Instilling in a child a sense of pride and identity is what will get them through all that life throws at them. Teaching them that happiness comes from within, not from having things, is what will teach them how to be fulfilled and happy even in times of crisis. Nathaniel Brandon stated, "The most important factor to consider when giving your child the basis for a happy adult life is to treat him with courtesy, respect, benevolence from the very beginning." That's all they need; not another Barbie Doll or Tonka truck. A portion of the lyrics in the song, "You Were Loved," sung by Whitney Houston, is: "You can have diamonds in your hands, have all the riches in the land; but without love, you don't really have a thing. When somebody cares that you're alive, when somebody trusts you with their life; that's when you know you have all you need. You'll hold this world's most priceless gift, the finest treasure that there is, when you can look back and know, you were loved." Craig knows he is loved. All children should be rich with love.

Some parents try to buy their children's love. Perhaps that is why many adults are in severe financial debt. Thousands of people a day in America file for bankruptcy. Were they never taught financial responsibility? Are they trying to buy friendships or love? Are they trying to buy happiness and fulfillment? Are they trying to compensate for what is lacking inside of them? I'm not sure what the motive is, but I would bet you they haven't been able to buy what they are searching for. Do children a favor and model delayed gratification. Model that the important things in life are free. Model decency, manners, consideration, kindness and generosity with one's compassion not one's wallet.

Children have the right idea. A little four year old in my class was so proud the day she wore a dress. Now this dress was about three sizes too big for her and looked like it had been around for years. But she didn't care. To her it was beautiful and she was beautiful in it. That's all that counts. In fact, her attitude did make the dress and her look absolutely stunning! That can't be bought.

Children don't care about bank accounts. They are taught that. Author Richard Carlson writes, "If you grew up in a family where there was a huge emphasis on money, where virtually every dinner conversation centred around the subject, you will have that information stored in your thought system. You will therefore be predisposed to placing an enormous emphasis on money yourself." This is not a formula to happiness. This teaches children all the wrong values. Children value feeling loved.

A good parent isn't regarded as such by their money. A good parent parents with love, nurturing, compassion and understanding. Too many children are getting lost in the dust of perceived success by their parents. It's easy to wrap yourself up in the pursuit of a successful business or project while putting off to another day the attention to dedicate to our children's needs. Lisa Whaley, in her book, <u>Reclaiming My Soul From the Lost and Found</u>, describes how she and her husband were driven to have successful careers, so they could "have it all." Her daughter's perspective was different. She would often tell her teachers, "Our family is different. My parents don't care what I do. Besides, they're never home anyway. They both work all the time." Lisa realized that her daughter "had already developed the perception that our work was more important to us than she was."

Is that extra dollar, or boat, or fancy car worth the price it may cost in the life of your child? Feeling accepted, supported and loved is more important than a big inheritance. Let your child know he is special, important and loved and he will be very wealthy indeed; and so will you! Now that's what matters! Craig knows that. Does your child?

Neale Donald Walsch also writes, "People loose their health to make money and then loose their money to restore their health." Don't fall into that trap. Be as wealthy as Craig's family and you won't need money.

Chapter Sixteen

Victoria

Victoria taught me- There)s no place like home and no one like Mom. And there shouldn't be.

I sometimes get too attached to the children in my class. It will surprise my colleagues to hear me admit this because I usually deny it. I have been known to call a family and ask to take their child for ice cream or to an event or just call to talk to them and ask how they're doing. I enjoy keeping connected with several kids and their families that have touched me over the years.

Victoria was one of those kids of whom I just couldn)t let go. She was like so many others in that she had several hardships in her life holding her back, but she had so much potential. She was smart, kind, beautiful, nurturing, and needy. Her mother had a low IQ and was near illiterate. She weighed approximately 450 pounds and found she received a lot of attention if she told lies, especially regarding her health. She once told us that she had cancer (which we discovered to be untrue). Then she said she had been pregnant with twins and they were born early so they died, but they were "them kind of babies that were connected at the head." She even told us the fictitious babies' names.

When Victoria was six years old, my husband and I were able to let her stay with us because her maternal grandfather was critically ill and Victoria's mom needed to help care for him. Victoria's older brother came periodically too, but mostly just Victoria. Victoria's home was very unclean and disadvantaged. This may seem like a value judgment on my part, but Victoria knew it too. In spite of this, Victoria developed a fondness for the attractive. She liked pretty things like hair clips, dresses, shoes, makeup, bows, etc. She didn〉t have much opportunity at home to receive these luxurious items, so I tried to provide her with a few preferred niceties while she stayed with us, including a pair of shoes. I thought they would still fit her the next summer and I asked, as she was packing her things to return home, if there was a place at her house she could keep the shoes until next summer. She said, (We'd better keep them here.) She knew.

While Victoria was in our care she experienced many firsts but the very first thing I had to do was get Victoria clean; so into the tub she went. While she soaked I took a soft nailbrush and scrubbed every inch of her grime-encrusted body. I had no idea so much crud could accumulate in the creases on the back of a child's knees. After I rid her hair of lice, I took her for her first hair cut at a real beauty salon. She was awkward as she glanced at her reflection in the mirror but even with her head tilted downward, she stretched the upper reaches of her beautiful soft eyes as she cautiously displayed a smile that reflected approval and pride. She looked endlessly in the mirror once home.

We, together with a friend who is the father of two very self-assured daughters, took her to an indoor playground/arcade. The expression on her face when we first walked in was priceless. Surprise and astonishment were all wrapped up in one beautiful expression. For the first half hour, or so, she was reluctant to go play without me right by her side but gained confidence as we were there, and began tunneling through the tubes just like all the other kids. Only occasionally did she need to run over for a reassuring hug then off she went again, smiling from ear to ear. On the way home, she asked if we could go there everyday. That would have been nice. We took her other places to gain new experiences, too. One such place was a nice restaurant. I think it was the first time she〉d ever eaten at a restaurant that wasn〉t adorned with a clown. I don〉t think she had ever seen such a variety of healthy food in all her life. She was reluctant to eat while anyone was watching so she snuck portions when she thought everyone was busy with their own meals. After we purchased her a bathing suit, I took her swimming at a real swimming pool. One of her favorite games was (dive for the penny;) possibly because she was amazed that she could see to the bottom of the pool.

She played dress-up in pretty, clean clothes. She commented how pretty they smelled and asked if I had sprayed them with perfume. I treasure the photos we have of her dressing up one of our flea-free dogs. She slept in a clean, nice smelling bed every night. She ate well-balanced home-cooked meals served on the dining room table during which we found ourselves needing to explain why we don't throw or spit unwanted food on the floor. She watched intently as I brushed my teeth. I don't think she had ever seen an adult brush their teeth before. We also discovered, using our sense of smell, that she had learned the habit of throwing used toilet paper in the trash instead of flushing it down the toilet. I guess their septic system, at home, was in such poor condition that it couldn't handle the extra load of paper products. She asked to have book after book read to her every night before bed. I am not listing the things we did to make us look like saints. I merely want to paint a picture for you of the opportunities Victoria had with us that she hadn't before experienced. We tried to anticipate and meet her every need. And she loved every experience, as did I.

I found I truly loved that little girl as I would if she were my own daughter. Her uncle and dying grandfather begged me to keep her. It was hard for me to explain and hard for us all to understand that if Victoria)s mom wanted her back, I had to return her, no matter what. I needed to be reminded of that as much as they needed to hear it. Victoria frequently spoke of her mom and asked if she could call her on the phone. I always assured her she could call her mom any time she wanted. One evening we were going over the agenda for the next days events, which included going to a county fair. Shortly after, Victoria stated her mom had taken them to a fair once. She began to look very sullen. I asked if she would like to phone her mom. While on the phone she repeatedly asked her mom if she wanted her to return home now. Her mom must have been saying, "No. You stay with MaryAnn," because Victoria tried to convince her mom that she needed her now. She told her mom things like, "if I come home I could clean the house for you and help you take care of Lenny and Grandpa and go to the store for you." When she hung-up the phone, she told me that her mom wanted her to go back home. I reassured her that she could go home any time she wanted. I gave her the option of going home now or after the fair. She repeated the story that her mom needed her home now. So, I knew it was time to take Victoria back home.

I couldn't imagine anyone wanting to return to that environment, but she was homesick. There's no place like home no matter what home is like. While driving the 42 miles north to her home, I spoke in a very upbeat voice trying to help mask my discontentment. When I asked what had been her favorite activity she said, "Everything!" Then she excitedly recapped all the events and activities she enjoyed while in our care. I stated that I'm sure her mom has missed her very much and would be so happy to see her. I reminded Victoria to use good manners and tell her mom how much she missed her when we arrived.

Just then we were pulling up her pothole infested, dirt driveway. The dogs that were tied outside were barking violently. Trying to put a positive spin on this seemingly senseless dissonance, I told Victoria they were barking because they were happy to see her. As we approached the old tarpaper structure, I could see a dim light through an open door. Before we even got to the doorway, a sickly sweet stench of rubbish forced me to hold my breath as it wafted toward us. It was the same odor that had forced me to put all the belongings with which Victoria arrived at my house directly into the clothes washer. But on Victoria's return to her home, she smelled pleasing in her clean new clothes and her professional new hairstyle. I hated to see her enter that dwelling and become contaminated by that aroma again. Every muscle and emotion in my body wanted to grab her and run as fast as I could to my car. But instead, I forced myself to walk closer to the open door of her indigent home. That's when I heard her mom say, in a very monotone voice, "Victoria's home." That was it, period. Once inside, her mom remained lying on the tattered couch that was propped up in the back with pieces of cement blocks. She didn)t get up to give Victoria hugs and kisses. She didn't excitedly say, "Oh Honey, I'm so glad your home. I've missed you so!" Just the seemingly unexcited, unmoving announcement, "Victoria's home."

Victoria skipped to a urine-stained mattress on the floor, which was between the undivided living room/kitchen, opened her suitcase and began showing it's contents to a neighbor girl that was there visiting. Seeing the neighbor girl reminded me of the unclean, disheveled appearance that Victoria donned before she came to our house. Being uncomfortable with the emotionless, quietness of the moment, I asked Victoria if she wanted to give her mom a kiss and tell her she missed her. She stoically walked over and gave a quick, stiff hug then ran back to the mattress. In her return route she passed the kitchen counter, which was overflowing with dirty dishes. I had noticed the dirty dishes shortly after we walked in but there was something odd about that heap that I couldn't quite figure out in the dim lighting. Then it became all too perfectly clear; as Victoria bumped the counter, a herd of flies frantically lifted from the dishes and scattered about. Seeing and hearing that many flies in one place actually startled me. I looked carefully at Victoria's reaction; that)s when I noticed she seemed different somehow. Studying her more attentively I noticed her head was drooping as she made sideways glances at her mom. What shocked me most, though, was her attitude. She had reverted to the unseen child, not wanting and cowering from attention.

Her beautiful smile that lit up my house was now a nervous tremble on one corner of her mouth. This little girl that had been so much a part of my life was now back in her domain; she didn't seem to fit and yet she did. Her cleanliness made her look out of place, yet it was apparent that life here was normal and comfortable to her. It was sad to watch all the self-confidence Victoria had developed drain from her body. All I could think of was the laughing, seemingly carefree child of just two hours ago. I thought in one panicked moment that I had to rescue her, so I asked her if she wanted to return home with me. I thought that the short visit may have been all she needed and she'd be ready to return home with me. From the pensive look on her face it was a difficult decision but she opted to stay home. It was time for me to go.

My heavy heart broke. I couldn't believe I had to leave her there. I cried so hard on the way home that I had to pull off the road several times to regain composure. I cried for her and for me. I had to keep reminding myself that no matter how much you love a child or how dismal their home is, there's no place like home and no one like Mom.

Mothers, please strive to be the best mom any child could possibly have. This doesn't mean give in to every wish and whim; give your child what he/she really needs. Therapists' couches are filled with adults who needed more from their parents. Not more toys. Not more money. Rather, more love. More nurturing. More understanding. More support. Moms are irreplaceable; no one can take your place.

I just watched the movie "A.I." The scientists thought they'd do humans a favor and create a robot child who could love. The prototype's mother rejected him and he wasn't capable of being reprogrammed to love another mother. He searched for 2000 years for his mother because he loved her. Nothing else mattered to him. He died wanting and searching for his mother. I think that movie accurately portrays the indestructible, undying love a child has for a parent. It is so important to not take for granted this special, powerful bond. I wasn't trying to take the place of Victoria's mom, although I did want to mother and nurture Victoria in ways she had not yet received. I wanted to impress upon her that there is another way of life. I wanted her to know what it feels like to be accepted, loved, confident, cuddled, clean, safe and secure. I wanted her to experience things she couldn't have otherwise. But I know now that she provided me with all that and more. However, I hope my early influence stays with her to help her meet her full potential. I'm not sure I'll ever know because the family moved to another state and I've lost contact with them.

So, wherever you are, Victoria, I hope you are well. I realize that you did more for me than I could ever do for you. You influenced my life forever and I will always love you. Thank you and God Bless You.

Chapter Seventeen

Collin

Collin taught me – you have to send them home.

His father was raising Collin, his older sister and younger brother. I don't remember what happened to the Mom. I think she just took off. Dad was doing the best he could. He had a paramour living with him. I don't think she appreciated being thrown into the instant role of mother of three.

Collin was the first little guy in my teaching career that I wanted to take home with me and keep forever and a day. He was three years old and had blonde hair so light that it was almost white and crystal green eyes.

Collin seemed to like coming to school more than he liked going home. This was apparent when he would resist getting his coat on when it was time to go home. The school day prior to dismissal showed no signs of resistance to any of our requests. On one day, in particular, Collin bucked more than usual during the preparation for dismissal. I took him aside and asked him if he wanted to tell me anything. He began to cry and through his tears said that he had wet the bed last night and was told that when he returned from school today he was going to get beaten and he would have to stay in his wet pajamas and wet bed the rest of the day and all night. After further questioning, I believed beyond a doubt that he was reporting accurately. I was crying right with him. I thought, "I just can't send this little boy home to this." I called our main office and asked what I could do. They reminded me that I could NOT keep this child at the center and should not report this to Children and Youth Services because it wasn't enough to go on. We saw no signs of abuse and couldn't be absolutely sure Collin was reporting accurately.

Frustrated, I returned to Collin. I tried to act reassuring and told him I would write a note to his "Mom." I wrote that Collin seemed stressed as he reported he wet the bed last night and could she please assure him that accidents happen and they would make sure they limited his liquid intake that evening so he could have a better chance of staying dry through the night tonight. I wasn't sure if the note would make things better or worse but I had to try. I didn't know what else to do.

I worried about that little boy all evening. The next day couldn't come quickly enough. I wondered if he would be sent to school that day or if he would have been "beaten" for his accident or if the letter had helped or if it further angered the parents.

I waited for the bus with pains in my stomach. I imagined they were similar to the pains that child must feel regularly. The pains of uncertainty are a helpless pain. It's so frustrating being held accountable for things over which we have no control.

Well, the bus pulled in and Collin was on board, smiling from ear to ear. He raced to hug me when he got off the bus. He said he did have to stay in his bed for a while but it was in dry clothes and a dry bed.

I thought maybe the mom learned to be a bit more understanding of the developmentally appropriate needs of a preschooler by this incident but returned to reality when she sent Collin and his sister to school very ill one day. His sister had a very high temperature. And was extremely lethargic. When we phoned to have the children picked up from school and taken home, no one answered. Nor could we contact any of the other people listed on the emergency forms. The poor kids had to suffer through the whole day at school. We made them as comfortable as possible, but they needed to be home to get proper rest. I sent a note home with them explaining how sick they were and should be kept home and possibly be seen by a doctor. Imagine my dismay when these children arrived on the bus the very next day. The sister was so ill that day that she literally couldn't stand. She told us her legs hurt and she didn't seem to have any strength in them at all. Her temperature was very high. Collin wasn't as ill but not well enough to participate in school activities, either. We called the mom and she said she didn't have transportation to come get the children. My teacher aide offered to drive these children home. (The aide had the foresight to take the thermometer with her to show the mom how high the fever had registered.) Upon her return, my aide reported that the mom was very displeased that these children were returned home.

All I could think to do was kidnap these kids. Since I knew that was not the answer, I decided the best thing I could do for these children is teach them to be as independent as possible and teach them basic survival skills. I taught them how to escape from a burning structure, how to dial and talk to the people at the emergency center, how to make a sandwich, pour their own drinks, how to properly wash their hair, how to dress appropriately for the weather, to look both ways before crossing a street, about stranger danger, ways to comfort themselves when feeling scared or lonely, to stay away from Mr. Yuck stuff, to practice safety around water and electric, and if you find a gun, walk away. All those important lessons necessary for safety, security and survival.

Other incidences occurred that year which did warrant CYS to investigate, but nothing major happened. I just hope the kids learned that no matter how they are treated that they are special and wonderful people and deserve to be treated well. Take care of yourselves, kids. I'll praying for you.

Chapter Eighteen

Oliver

Oliver taught me .... Go with my gut feeling.

Oliver was one of seven children residing in a mobile home with their father and his paramour. Oliver was delayed in his cognitive, verbal and physical development. He was a lovable, shy, withdrawn little boy who seemed oblivious to his surroundings. During meals he would eat disproportionately large amounts of food in an animal-like manner. He hovered over his plate and quickly scooped food into his mouth. He ate so quickly that I didn't know if he took time to chew or breath. It was common for him to eat such large quantities that he would vomit soon after eating. It seemed as if he hadn't eaten anything in two days. Being concerned with this, I spoke to his dad, who explained that Oliver had an eating disorder. It seemed funny, however, that no matter how often I requested documentation from doctors concerning this alleged disorder, Oliver's dad could never produce it or remember the name of the disorder.

Oliver was frequently absent from school and upon his return often harbored a variety of bruises. When I'd ask him how he got that "boo-boo? He would say, «I dunno» or nothing at all. Once in a while he would state, «Dad» in his usual aloof manner. That alone wasn't enough to indicate who was the perpetrator of the abuse, if it was indeed abuse. His dad was always quick with an explanation for the bruises, though. Since Oliver had poor motor skills the «accidents,» as Dad would call them, seemed almost believable. Almost.

I just knew something wasn't right. Every time I evaluated the situation I deducted that Oliver was the perfect candidate for a victim of abuse. He was small. He couldn't fight back. He was clumsy. All his communication skills were delayed. His vocabulary was limited and his comprehension skills were questionable. The only thing I could do was document every suspicion I had. I spoke to the appropriate authorities within our own school system. That person did everything she was mandated to do. We were both afraid that if we pushed too hard, the dad would pull Oliver out of our program. Then he would have no explaining to do to anyone and he would definitely get away with the abuse we suspected he was inflicting. But we couldn't just sit back and watch this child repeatedly have suspicious marks on him. That wasn't helping anyone.

My fears about this family were further heightened, because Oliver's sister had been in my class a couple years prior and I suspected something wasn't quite right with her, either. She seemed depressed and uncomfortable with smiling. She would nervously look around before resuming an activity. The only time she played with someone else was when she created an imaginary friend. She often carried a baby doll and quietly told it, "It's okay. I'll take care of you." And asked the baby doll, «Are you hurt?" It all seemed odd but no definite signs of abuse.

With Oliver, though, there were just too many signs pointing to abuse. One time Oliver's back was so littered with bruises that I photographed it. The photo showed numerous bruises from neck to buttocks in a varying degree of coloration. This indicated injuries occurring at different times. In other words this kid was getting battered on a regular, if not daily, basis. We did all we could do to document and report our suspicions again to the county authorities. Nothing ever happened. I worried about that boy all summer when our program wasn't in session. I couldn't help but think that we had failed him.

Then that fall all my fears came painfully true. An old neighbor of theirs reported to me that Oliver had indeed been the victim of his dad's frequent drunken rage. I instantly became sick to my stomach. I was so mad and disappointed in myself. I questioned myself relentlessly. Why didn't I do more? Why didn't I take that photo and slam it on the caseworker's desk at children and youth services or the police? Why didn't I try to build a better rapport with the family and possibly do some intervention and education myself? Why wasn't something done?

I wanted answers so I called the assigned reporter within my agency and reported what I had just heard. Her voice contained the same anger and sorrow that I was feeling but her words reminded me that the report I had just heard was hearsay. Her explanation was probably meant to help relinquish us from the guilt. But my guilt was deep and lasting. I couldn't help thinking that I could have been the one to save this little boy from continued pain and suffering, the likes of which I'm sure I've never seen, and never want to. I couldn't imagine his life of awakening every day to the possibility of being hungry all day and wondering when the next blow was going to strike.

A couple months later our local paper reported domestic abuse in this home. The dad had physically assaulted the paramour. I hoped this was a sign that dad had hit bottom and would be mandated to attain assistance and get his act together, but no such luck. A couple years later I read with despair the report that one of Oliver's older brothers had drowned in a needless accident. I felt sorry for the family but I wasn't so sure I felt sorry for the boy. He was now free from abuse. He no longer had to help dad stagger in the door late at night and play "Go find the car." This was a ritual, the neighbors explained to me, in which the kids would have to walk the road in search of their dad's car, which was in a ditch or in some other abandoned position because that's all the farther the dad could manage to drive it home that night. At that point, he would stumble home and order the young boys to drive the car home or walk to neighbors to ask them to drive the car home. This happened all hours of the night, which meant the boys, the oldest of which was around nine years old, were often pulled from their beds to carry out this adult responsibility. Then who knows what they had to deal with once they returned home.

I wish I had fought harder to protect Oliver. Maybe I could have saved him from another beating and saved his brother from drowning. Maybe all the children could have had a better chance at being productive, well-adjusted adults. My friends and colleagues remind me that I can't save the world. But couldn't I have saved this one child?

In my meager attempt to save one child at a time, I have decided I would like to take a stand toward changing the vague laws governing this area. Often action cannot be taken in the best interest of a child because the law is written as to protect against what is considered, value judgments. I have discovered Pennsylvania law states that letting a child live with a head polluted with lice is not neglect but rather a value judgment. I can't believe that! What about the undeniable damage done to a child's self-esteem when ostracized because of the cronic infestation of these bugs? I know our local agencies are extremely under funded and they have to operate understaffed. This needs to change. How about using some of the money being handed out to research things, such as how fast different ketchups pour from their bottle for child welfare programs. This is a priority for the future of our entire country. How are these abused, scared, insecure children going to grow up to be healthy productive adults? The answer is: they aren't! Statistics show that nearly every neglected child will be dependent on our society his/her entire life. They will have low self-esteem and have no suitable role models. One of my past evaluations stated that I don't like all the red tape one must follow in our job. That's right. I don't. When something is wrong, it's wrong. When the best interest of a child is at stake there shouldn't be any hoops to jump through or t's to cross or red tape to cut through; let common sense rule and just do the right thing. «Just do it" should be the motto of working with children instead of a shoe company. Foot work needs done but not for one's own health but rather for the health and well being of children, our society and the future of all. I tried to become more conforming over the years because I thought that is what I should do. You know the speech: "Don't ruffle any feathers," and "Don't step on any toes." I know sometimes I have to conform or I would go around with a big chip on my shoulder and be ready to fight at the drop of a hat. I don't mean to be a rebel without a cause, but I'm going with my gut feeling from now on. I'm going to fight for what I know is right for a child and instead of keeping quiet so as to not cause trouble for authority. Maybe I can't save the world~ but if I can save just one child from enduring what Oliver has, it will be worth it.

Chapter Nineteen

Carlie

Carlie taught me............. Children internalize and personalize.

Carlie is now an adult but she told me a story from when she was five years old. Her parents weren't getting along very well and argued frequently. During one such argument, she overheard her mother shout to her dad that she wished she had never married him and that she wasn't happy anymore. Five-year-old, Carlie, internalized this statement and evaluated in her young mind that if Mommy hadn't married Daddy, she would never have been born. She concluded that Mommy must not want her and isn't happy that she was born. No five year old can articulate any of this. They don't yet possess that skill. But this one incidence, when she was five-years-old, left such an impression on Carlie that she can painfully recall the story and all the feelings that accompanied it so long ago. Internalizing the events, definitely left a negative imprint on her very being. It negatively wrote on the slate of who she is, as Dr. Phil, psychologist and author, would say. It affected her value as a person and her self-esteem.

Dr. Phil explains that no one's behavior happens in a vacuum. It affects everybody in the vicinity - particularly kids. When children hear arguments, they don't forget them. They may never speak of them but they will inventory them. That puts stock in their developing behavior as to how one behaves and chooses to handle life's situations. It fossilizes in their characters. Children should not be totally shielded from conflicts, even between their parents. This teaches them that it is normal to become less than pleased with someone you love, but it also teaches them how to effectively handle these conflicts and get past these temporary feelings. The opportune word in the previous sentence is "effectively." If parents are not dealing well with conflict, it will confuse and upset children. If parents fight just to fight, without resolution, children will be taught to live in a world of unproductive interactions. This will affect them negatively and all those around them. If conflicts are handled effectively, children will learn the distiction of not liking what someone is doing over not liking someone, period. They will learn the balance between give and take and learn to compromise. They will learn it is possible to be angry at what someone has done other than being angry at that person; and in fact, still love that person. This enables a child to feel secure in the fact that she is still loved even though someone isn't happy with what she did. There is a great children's book titled, "Mama, Do You Love Me?" by Barbara M. Joossee. This is a must in a children's library. It explains that even though Mama is angry, she still loves her "Dear One" because a parents love is forever. Children need to personalize and internalize this above all else. It is essential.

Not feeling loved, unconditonally, is a grossly apparent reason for a permenant scar to occur in a child but permanent emotional scars can occur from smaller instances in a child's life, just as well. Nathaniel Brandon wrote in the Six Pillars of Self-Esteem, "Not all manifestations of non self-assertiveness are obvious. The average life is marked by thousands of unremembered silences surrenders, capitulations and misrepresentations of feelings and beliefs that corrode dignity and self-respect." The self-fulfilling prophecy shines true here. If a child is told he/she is "stupid," he/she feels, "I may as well do poorly in school because my parents think I'm stupid anyhow." The child may not consciously know why she is choosing to do poorly, it's just a feeling imprinting on her personality.

Maxwell Maltz in his book, Psycho-cybernetics and Self-fulfillment tells two stories of this very concept. During a session with a patient, the patient told him something that had obsessed him all his life. "In school, as a youngster, a teacher had said he was stupid, and that he would never amount to anything. He had never forgotten this teacher's remark, and had adopted this critical attitude toward himself. After this, he had done poorly in school. He finally dropped out of school. And ever since, he had considered himself a failure." Another example he cites is, "Helen, seven, overheard her parents say, on hearing her play the piano, that she was clumsy with her hands and would never become a good pianist. She accepted this as the truth and whenever she played the piano she played clumsily to confirm the truth of what her parents had said." Maltz said to her, "My dear child, you can't be held responsible for the actions of someone else even if they are your parents." Two years later she played the piano well.

I heard a disturbing story of how words can give a child the wrong impression of herself. My friend asked an acquaintance of hers if she'd taken her eight year-old shopping with her the day before. The mom answered, right in front of the child, "I'd rather have needles stuck in my eyes!" I shudder to realize what that statement did to the psyche of that child. It makes me ill just to hear it; I can't imagine how ill it made the innocent little child feel. Statements like that have long lasting affects on the very being of a child. It truly changes who they are, their self-perception and who they become. Famous football player, Joe Namath, states half-heartedly, "Until I was 13, I thought my name was 'shut-up.' I'm afraid a lot of children feel that way. It's a shame. Never believe the old children's rhyme of "sticks and stones can break my bones, but words will never hurt me." They do hurt. And those hurts don't heal the way a broken bone does. Those hurts don't mend, they blend into what we think about ourselves thus who we become.

Children think the world revolves around them. It's very difficult for them to see outside themselves. That's why they internalize and personalize everything. They feel it has to be about them because they are the center of everything. That is why some seemingly harmless statements are potentially damaging. Since I have been aware of this, I have been very conscious of statements made around children that could be misinterpreted and internalized in a negative way. Statements that have become common, and said without the intent to inflict scars in a child, but can be wounding non-the-less. Statements like, "I don't want to deal with it anymore." That's like telling your kids, "I don't want to deal with YOU anymore." Well, don't be surprised when your kids don't want to deal with YOU anymore. A child should never get the impression of being unwanted. I understand all parents get stressed, it goes with the territory, but you still can't say phrases like, "I'm sick and tired of all this." The child will interpret it as, "Mommy is sick and tired of me." Not a good feeling for a little one to harbor. That damaging feeling goes deeper than any visible scar ever could. Consider the expression, "You are going to be the death of me." Can you imagine if, God forbid, something tragic were to happen to the adult that uttered that sentiment to a child? That poor little child will always feel she was the cause of the adult's death. She will eternally think that if she hadn't misbehaved, that person would still be alive. What an awful burden for a child to carry through life, even if it's only subconsciously. Another common statement is, "She just doesn't listen." You have just informed that child that you don't expect her to listen. She will internalize that and transfer that thinking to, 'Nobody listens to me. I mustn't be worth listening to." When a child internalizes that impression of herself, she becomes an extremely withdrawn child or a severely behavior problem child.

I recently overheard a mom responding to her daughter's preference to quit taking dance classes. The mom said, "Good! I'm tired of sitting there while she takes her lesson." Wow! Let's think about all the implications of that statement. The main one that concerns me is the insinuation that the child isn't worth waiting for or supporting.

Some anorexics state that they grew up in a house where money was tight and the mom was always worried about having enough money for even the basics like food. So the child felt guilty for eating any of the food because that would have caused more stress on their mom. Some anorexics state that they felt like they weren't worth the food they might consume. Something was said to these people, right or wrong, intentioned or not, that left them the impression that they aren't worth the food they needed to consume.

My friend witnessed children exiting their building from another day at school. One little girl ran up to her mom to share some news of the day with her and the mom's response was, "Get out of my face!" I have to wonder who that little girl will turn to next time she wants to share, good or bad news. Or let's fast-forward six to seven years when this little 14-15 year old is being faced with young teen pressures. Who is she going to share her fears, worries and desires with? I bet not someone who has given her the message that she should stay out of sight. No doubt when this little girl wants to be "seen," she will act-out in such an extreme way that the mom will have no choice than to have her "in her face." Hopefully, she won't be looking at that face behind bars or lying in a hospital bed or at a pregnancy clinic.

My neighbors returned from a week's vacation. Immediately upon pulling into their driveway, the children were at my house asking if they could stay overnight. I told them that even though they are home, this is still their vacation time with their family and maybe they should spend the night at home as a family. When the little girl told her mom this, the mom declared, "We've had enough family time." So when a child internalizes this, the interpretation becomes, "I've had more than enough time with you!" Not exactly a message one should convey to their child. The children stayed overnight at my house that night. I thought it was important for them to be with someone who could let them know, beyond a shadow of a doubt, that they are wanted, today and always.

These are just some examples of the "Thousands of unremembered silences and misrepresentations of feelings and beliefs that corrode dignity and self-respect." When a persons dignity is corroded, she will not demand respect from others. She will feel she deserves all the bad stuff that comes her way.

Robert M. Williams, author of the book, <u>The Missing Peace In Your Life</u> states, "Research shows that we are most programmable from conception to about age 6. During that time we have little or no faculty of conscious discernment. That is to say, as young children we possess limited capability to put into proper perspective harsh, critical, or mean-spirited comments directed toward us by parents, siblings, schoolmates, or adult authority figures. In effect, we take everything personally. It is this early lack of discernment that creates the mental software that makes up the foundation of our adult personalities."

In my family, I have four sisters and one brother. It seemed the boy child was always more valued. I can't repeat exact statements that have caused me to come up with that conclusion but apparently subtle statements were made, throughout my childhood, to drive that message home to me. I'm sure statements and actions were not intentionally said or done to make me feel less of a valued human being just because I am a girl, but that is what I personalized and internalized.

I heard a lady, about 55 years old, speak about how she internalized her dad's behavior from her childhood and how it left impressions that has impeeded her throughout her adulthood. She started out by saying, "I never thought things that happened so many years ago could affect me or impact me today; 'cause my life should be pretty good." She tells the following story: "My parents divorced when I was 10. The judge wanted her to make a decision about who to live with. I desperately wanted to live with Mom 'cause I was afraid of my dad. But Dad said, 'You gotta come live with me or I won't be able to make it. I'm not gonna live.' So I moved in with Dad. I had to come straight home from school everyday to clean. One day, Dad slammed the door in my face. I cried so hard I could hardly catch my breath. And then, at 15 years old, when he didn't like something I said, he would slap me. Once I asked if I could go to the fair in Lexington with friends. He didn't slap me - he punched me out to the kitchen and against a wall in the hall, then walked away. He just walked away. I didn't know what to do.

I frequently thought "that is my dad. Obviously I had to have done something wrong for him to have done that to me. I just couldn't figure out what it was; 'cause dads don't do that to his kids. It had to be me!"

That's what children come away with. A sense of guilt and shame and feelings that they must deserve this kind of treatment. That underlying guilt and shame doesn't end just because we chronologically age. It affects adult relationships. It usually is replicated into adult life. What happens to us at four 10, 15 years old, relates to how we treat ourselves as adults and how we tolerate being treated.

I read the poem by Danny Comstock entitled, "Words of Love?" It was derived from conversations he had with women who survived abusive relationships and, fortunately, gained courage to leave. I couldn't help but wonder if they were able to tolerate this demeaning way of life for so long because it was just a continuation of what they were used to from their childhood. The poem makes statements a child should never hear, but too many children do; and start to believe it about themselves. This leads the way to being tolerant of slanderous statements as adult. The poem states: "You're fat! You're ugly! You're nothing but a bitch! Clean the house! Take care of the kids! Can't you do anything right? You're not sexy! You don't turn me on! You're frigid, cold as ice! You don't appreciate my love! Why I put up with you, I don't understand! But no one will understand you like I do! You need me to take care of you! You won't survive without me! If you don't listen to me, I will hit you again! Then you will understand how much I love you!" If these kinds of statements wear down an adult, can you imagine what they do to a child's developing sense of being? It makes them believe they are what they have been told. The old saying of, "you are what you eat" is very true. It is also true that we are what we have been told to believe about ourselves. Don't let anyone feed negativity to children. Of course we can't protect a child from everything that is said and done in their presence but we can control what goes on in a child's own home.

Dr. Phil accurately states that a child's home has got to be their soft place to fall. They've got to know no matter what else happens in this world, there are two people who think, "I'm the most special thing that's ever come down the road," They've got to feel this. They've got to internalize this with absolute certainty. If they know this, they can better ward off all the potentially damaging words and actions inflicted upon them and still keep their integrity intact.

The following fairy tale explains how quickly and innocently a series of events can lead to a lifetime of what we say to ourselves:

> Once upon a time there were two young children who possessed beautiful, gentle, old souls. The little girl decided to take dance lessons after watching a recital in which a friend participated a year prior.
>
> This little girl worked beyond her years to remember where her hands were to go in correlation to her feet. This task is usually developed around ages 8-10. The fact that this young prodigy had been using her appendages for only seven years, made this task even more difficult.
>
> This precious little girl went to dance every week. Sometimes she didn't want to go because she wanted to be doing something else and sometimes because she was tired. The concept of needing to practice

every week in order to slowly develop needed skills for a far away goal was difficult for her to understand; but once at class, she always danced her huge heart out.

As the night of the big dance recital approached, she worked harder than ever before to remember and coordinate all those moves. The morning after dress rehearsal, she called an older trusted friend. She expressed that she had felt nervous while on the stage during rehearsal. The wise friend pulled from her years of experience to try to relieve her prodigy's case of stage fright by explaining to her that she should embrace those butterflies in her stomach and not fear them because those feelings are there to let her know that she is excited and challenged. In fact, those very feelings are what will help her get through it. "Just remember to focus and smile when you get those feelings." The friend told her. This advice seem to comfort her nerves and strengthen her determination.

The long awaited night came. She had been up later than usual the night before and was also feeling anxieties about the family's preparations for vacation the next day. The rain that had drenched the incoming audience could not dampen the spirit of this little dancer. When her dance troop strolled down the side aisle, she scanned the sea of faces for familiar, reassuring, comforting, approving ones. She seemed relieved to see her family and mentor sitting there in proud anticipation. It was evident she was nervous as she approached that stage, but forged ahead and performed the required moves. It was splendid.

As the family and mentor appreciated the performance of others, they were truly just putting in time until their special little dancer graced the floor again. " Oh! There she is again!" rushed automatically out of the mouth of the mentor as her eyes filled with tears with the little one's second entrance to the stage. The outward portrayal of dance was dimmed by her inner beauty. The mentor only hoped her little one was as proud of herself as she was of her. What a gracious young lady. It was hard to believe this was the same girl that needed to be reminded endlessly to stop making ugly, crass, burping sounds.

Her little brother, who had just sat very well through almost three hours of dance, without a snack or drink, was even proud of her. When it was all over, he helped the mentor pass what seemed to be a long time but was surely only about 15 minutes until the little dancer could be in their congratulatory arms. It was a perfect evening....... until the photo session that followed.

What started out as some innocent picture taking to capture this momentous occasion, turned into the ruin of an evening, leaving lasting imprints on two souls and the crashing of a little girl's dream. Surrounded by the community, fellow dancers, their families and her own family members, she and her dripping with pride father waited patiently with a smile for the camera. Her mom, embarrassed because she couldn't figure out how to work the new camera, began to berate and humiliate the dad. This tired little princess's proud posture slowly slouched and a frown replaced her once smiling face. As if this hadn't been enough poison already, the mom demanded, as she lined up for a photo with her tired daughter, "Get my picture with her. I'm the one who did all the work." This once beaming little dancer briefly looked at her mom in confused disbelief but quickly and obediently looked at the camera. Her pride wilted more. Then the mom yelled loudly at the little boy because he didn't release from a hug as quickly as she thought he should. That little dancer looked like she wanted to crawl under a seat. The joy of getting the siblings in one picture was quickly robbed when the now extremely impatient mom, grabbed the reluctant, tired little boy by the arm and proceeded to spanked him on his bottom. That's right! In front of everyone. Yea, that will make him want to smile and cooperate and conform! To put icing on the cake, the mom then blamed her actions on the little boy and declared that HE had just ruined the whole evening. The helpless little boy looked for comfort and for someone to help him make sense of what just occurred. If he could have expressed himself, he would have said, "What the Hell just happened here. I'm hungry, tired, bored, and need taken care of; not publicly humiliated and made to feel worse. Doesn't anyone care about my needs and wants and desires? I'm just a little boy. What do you expect?" This internal dialog would have been parroted by his sister with the addition of, "I just wanted to have a nice evening. Does this kind of thing always have to happen? I was having the time of my life but now, I just want to go." The lonely silhouette of that sad little boy, that had been rescued by his dad, could be seen languishing away in one direction. The other direction revealed that once proud little girl, independently dragging herself to the car with her mom, and her glory was over. That is the memory this little girl will carry with her for the rest of her life of her first dance recital."

Who knows if she'll ever dance again? Who knows what messages she walked away with? Who knows what she internalized from that night? Certainly not the sparkle and pride she should have. These instances leave such a mark on the subconscious. I'm sure she will never be able to put her finger on it and tell what impression it left on her; she'll just feel it, forever. Only time will tell the extent to which this stole a piece of her eternal happiness. A friend of mine once said, "How can you expect wholeness and love from a broken heart?" How can this child be whole or generously give love from a broken heart? Once a heart is broken, it can be glued back together, but it's still an impaired heart. It will never be the same. That's internal damage that will erode the core of a person's chance for peace. What an awful thing to steal from a child.

Everything that happens around a child influences who they are and who they will become. We need to protect a child's perception of herself that is molded by her surroundings. Robert M. Williams also states, "Beliefs establish the limits of what we can achieve. It is especially true when the beliefs are subconscious. Our behaviors are a direct reflection of our beliefs, perceptions, and values, generated from past experiences." Instill in children that they can achieve anything. Instill in them to require others to treat them with respect and dignity. Instill in them a confidence in their own value. These are the basic foundations that a child needs to internalize and personalize.

Chapter Twenty

Levi

Levi taught me – Parents do what they can.

Levi was a beautiful boy with dark hair and large brown eyes. His missing front tooth could be seen only on the infrequent occasion he displayed his beautiful dimpled smile. His hair always needed combed and he wore dingy, worn clothes that rarely fit correctly. He resided with two siblings, mother and step-dad. His mom and step-dad both worked menial jobs outside the home which meant money was always tight. It was apparent that the family lacked basic necessities and comforts. I could understand that there was never enough money to go around but I sometimes wondered why they didn't just clean things up. I remember thinking, a can of Comet costs only 48 cents. You can clean just about anything with Comet. When I got to know the family better, I learned to look past the dirt and deeper into their accomplishments in difficult times.

The mom took me in her confidence about some family matters and hardships, both past and present. I then realized that it's not as important whether one is wearing clean clothes but rather, has clothes to put on at all. It's not important if the house is clean when the family is facing being homeless or at the very least, cold and hunger. Yes, this happens in America, folks - in our backyards. Everyday! When one has to worry about where the family is going to live day-to-day, nothing else is a priority. When a worn, torn structure is the only place one can call home, it's better than nothing. Supervising a homework assignment doesn't seem as important as working an extra hour so there will be money for gas in the car to get to work the next day. Scrubbing the floor takes a back seat to making endless phone calls in an attempt to attain home heating oil, especially when it's 20 degrees outside and there is only enough oil in the tank for three more days (if the thermostat is kept at 60 degrees, that is). When parents are worried that they won't have enough food to feed the kids the next day it makes "sleep tight" take on a whole new meaning. I'm sure their dreams include delights like having hot water and money that stretches enough for toiletries; an adequate supply of food; a warm outfit for everyone; and a clean bed in a safe and secure environment. These same parents just cannot worry if Levi is sharing well or brushing his teeth properly or learning his ABC's. They just don't have the strength left to worry about these things. It doesn't make them bad parents, just overwhelmed parents in every real sense of the word. Overwhelmed does not mean getting little Johnny to hockey practice after school and picking up Suzie for dance class before the dog would need to be taken out. We're talking painful reality here. The reality of stretching what's already thin, one more day, in order to survive is what I'm talking about.

I tutored for a while in a homeless shelter. I learned the importance of teaching kids skills most of us take for granted. Such as, where to call "home;" secrets to keep and which ones may harm someone if kept; how to feel good about oneself, especially under these stressful conditions; how to feel a part of anything; how to feel a sense of belonging and ownership. One routine we established quickly, when new residents moved in, was to determine where to put one's belongings. In the cramped shelter that often meant the child had a chair or a corner to claim as theirs. That was it. But the children were happy for that and protected and retreated to that personal space as though it were a luxurious spacious palace.

I learned to not judge these folks. They are doing the best with what they have. Their circumstances dictate what kind of parents they can be. Their hearts are in the right place. They don't love their children any more or less than people with abundant material wealth. They just have to worry more.

Margie Chalofsky, Glen Finland and Judy Wallace state in the book, Changing Places, A Kid's View Of Shelter Living, that children in the middle of family crisis often see themselves as essentially different from other children. They feel that they alone have been chosen for these burdens and that there must be something wrong with them. They may also feel responsible. We need to teach that although all children do not share the same experiences, all children do share a common humanity and are to be treated with dignity and friendship. If you are a teacher, you can make the difference between whether school becomes a place for a child to feel ashamed or accepted, alienated or included...." One nine-year-old resident of a shelter stated, "One girl asked me where I lived, but I didn't tell her. I got scared she'd think 'cause we're homeless that Mom's lazy or doesn't take care of us. But that's not true. My Mom wants to work again. She's trying hard to get another job." Normal needs of children turn into a nightmare for parents under these trying conditions. Roberto, a 12 year old, was sad when he expressed, "I made Mama cry today, and I feel bad. I just had to tell her I needed new shoes 'cause my sneakers had holes in them. She started crying and said she couldn't take care of me..." A worker at the shelter, who had witnessed said, "tell your Mama that being a good mother is about loving and not about money for sneakers." One boy, age 13, stated, "Mom acted like she didn't even hear anything. She's so worried about her own problems, she ignores me now." I'm sure she heard, she just didn't have any strength left to respond. My friend, Deborah, when describing her upbringing, said about her mother, "It wasn't that she didn't want to be a good mom. She had her own problems and just didn't have time to deal with mine. She did what she had to do for us all to survive." When a person is at their limit, ignoring becomes a basic survival technique. When you've given all, you have nothing left to give even if you want to.

Students can become very apprehensive, develop school phobias, have a drop of self-esteem and neglect or totally ignore their school work when living under these conditions. My friend, Deborah, states that she turned to shoplifting under these trying conditions. She thought it was a way of helping her overburdened mom and struggling family. When she got caught, the only reason her mom was angry was because it was one more thing with which to deal. Usually the parents are tending to other problems and can't worry how their children are feeling about all the changes being thrust upon them.

Since parents are already doing their best maybe the best way to assist families through their tough times is to take an interest in their lost children. This can increase their self-esteem because someone cares and is paying attention to them; and then maybe they won't need quite as much from their parents, which will free the parent to focus their energy on doing what they can to get the family out of these monumentally weighty situations. They are doing everything they can. Deborah found another family to take an interest in her when she was feeling lost. She remembers her mother saying, "Just leave me alone." So she did. She moved out when she was 13 years old. Her mom was very hurt. Deborah did not do this to hurt her mom but to find a family where she didn't feel pushed away, and didn't have to steal anymore.

Instead of looking from the outside and thinking, it's not good enough, I try to help. All anyone can do is their best. If it doesn't appear as though they are, maybe they just need some help. The song, "People" talks about this. Come on, I know you know it, sing along with me, but pay close attention to the message the words convey. "People. People who need people, are the luckiest people in the world. Where children, needing other children and yet letting our grown-up pride, hide all the need inside, acting more like children than children." Put pride aside, see all the needs inside, and help where you can. Hopefully the parents are going through, only a temporary setback. When they get back on their feet, their child can be standing right with them.

Chapter Twenty-one

Izaak

Izaak taught me – Parents need a safe place to learn, too.

Izaak was an only child to Maria, a teen mother, and a 50-something dad. The mother had been in special needs classes throughout her schooling. She functioned at the level of a fourth grader. She was raised by parents who were from the old school of spare the rod, spoil the child. They barked commands at children instead of speaking to them. They were a rough and rugged group of folks.

When Maria turned 18, she and her boyfriend and their two year old, Izaak, moved into their own house together. Maria wanted to convey that even though she was young, she took good care of her family. She bragged about how she always had dinner cooked for her boyfriend when he returned home from work. She had a good heart and really wanted to be doing the right things for her family, especially her little boy. She just didn't know what all that entailed because she never had good parenting role models.

When Izaak started school at age three, Maria rode the bus with him everyday. It was quickly evident that she was coming to school because she wanted to learn, too. We began to see Maria blossom the first week. Her tone of voice softened and she smiled all the time. She LOVED school. She cried the day Izaak developed diarrhea and they had to leave school early. Another sign of her devotion to school was Maria's familiarity with the children in the class. She was startled when she returned after a couple days absence and met a newly enrolled child. I think she was offended that we hadn't checked with her first. But she quickly accepted and became comfortable with that child, too.

I think this was the most positive school experience Maria ever had. She was excited and proud when she knew the answers and could cut or draw better than the students. My teacher aid and I strived to find ways she could feel useful.

After about two weeks of school, our cook asked me if that mom bothered us in the classroom. I said, "Yes, a bit, but she really needs to be here every bit as much as her son and she is making great progress." This was the best place she could be to learn how to be a more tender, nurturing, patient mom and learn age appropriate expectations of her son. In many ways it was like having another child in the class. She learned, right along with her son, how to and when to properly wash hands, how to eat with utensils, to use tissues for blowing one's nose instead of one's shirt, to say, "please" and "thank you," how to wait for your turn, not to swear, to not interrupt others when they are talking, and a whole multitude of other life skills.

In January of Izaak's first year we had a meeting with his parents about Izaak's development. Izaak was three years, four months old at that time and functioning at the level of a one-and-a-half-year-old overall. Maria and her boyfriend accepted that news okay but then the bomb was laid. The special needs teacher suggested that Maria no longer volunteer in Izaak's classroom to promote learning from his peers and teachers; and become more independent of his mother. This recommendation was made because Izaak gravitated to his mom as a playmate instead of his peers and Maria would speak for Izaak instead of encouraging him to speak for himself. No matter how we explained it, I could tell that Maria was upset about that news. I assured her that she could still come to school but her help was needed in the other classroom or the kitchen. She began to cry. I reminded her that her little boy was growing up and although it's hard to let them go, Izaak deserved the chance to be on his own. I commended her for being a caring mom and empathized with her when explaining that sometimes it's hard to realize that it's not good to mother them too much. I patronized her by saying she would be missed and we wouldn't know what to do without her in our classroom. I assured her that we would allow her to come give Izaak a hug frequently, if she needed it, but then we'd direct her back to the other room. I encouraged her by telling her that the other classroom teacher was excited about having her in her room to help because they know she is such a great helper.

The next day at school, I greeted Maria, gently but firmly and guided her to the other classroom. We both giggled and off she went. I'm sure it was hard on her to see Izaak doing so well each time she peeked in our classroom. It's a difficult realization that we need our kids more than they need us.

Izaak progressed in leaps and bounds the rest of that year and so did Maria. I congratulate Maria for learning to give her little boy space to grow. I also congratulate Maria for seeing a great opportunity for herself to grow, and grab a hold of it. She even began attending the adult computer classes held upstairs in our building.

Many of the employees in our federally funded program are women who once had a child in our program. They appreciated too the opportunity of going back to school. This gave them the chance to pass from one stage of experience to graduating into the workforce. It a wonderful program and a wonderful opportunity for the children and their parents. I'm honored and proud to be a small part of the process.

Chapter Twenty-two

Mitchell

Mitchell taught me --- You can lead a child to food but you can't make him eat!

During Mitchell's first year in my class, he displayed a bit of a temper, especially when he couldn't get his own way. In protest, he would shout, "I never comin' 'ack ta 'cool." That's not a typo; he had a speech delay. Of course, two minutes later he would be smiling and hugging staff. During Mitchell's second year in my class, he was usually a pleasant and obedient child, except one trait remained consistent: Mitchell almost never ate our food. His older sister, who had been in my class two years prior to him, was a selective eater too, but nothing compared to Mitchell. Pediatric nutritionist claim that a new food needs to be introduced 15 times before a child will like it and perhaps develop a taste for that particular food. Mitchell proved them all wrong.

At our school, we have one of the most wonderful cooks in the history of cafeteria-style food. Her sinfully delicious homemade rolls make us salivate as we anxiously await their warm exit from the oven. Since I have been a vegetarian for years, our cook, whose name is also Mary Ann, rose to the challenge of preparing some foods in a new way, to be sure I had something to eat, especially on stinky tuna days. She took pride in feeding everyone and making sure no one left hungry.

Sometimes it seems like all we do at preschool is eat. Within two hours, we have lunch and snack. I typically gain 10-15 pounds every school year because delicious food is so easily available that I eat even when I'm not hungry. This means I spend the summer working it off . We are encouraged to eat with the children to facilitate a "family-style" atmosphere of eating while working on children's self-help skills and socialization skills. The abundance of good food and the great atmosphere made Mitchell's lack of consuming our food even more puzzling.

Mitchell even stopped eating our hot dogs at school because he said they "smelled different" than Grandma's. He wouldn't eat our macaroni and cheese for the same reason. He would eat grilled cheese sandwiches but not unmelted cheese on cheese and cracker days. His limited choices lead to him to just sitting at mealtime and staring at his plate while ingesting only milk. Mitchell's current choice of foods consists of sweets, junk foods and processed foods; absolutely no fruits or vegetables and only hot dogs and chicken nuggets in the meat department. The likely consequences of Mitchell's sugary, processed food choices is that he will weigh 300 pounds by the time he graduates from High School and have heart disease and diabetes. I sure hope he proves me wrong. Chef Bobo, author of <u>Chef Bobo's Good Food Cookbook</u> states that, "The reason we're having problems today with diabetes in kids is because there's corn syrup in everything. It may mean ketchup! Ketchup has more sugar in it than ice cream." I knew it was important to try to teach Mitchell to eat a healthier diet.

I tried all the standard procedures on Mitchell for encouraging a child to eat – I'd praise all the other children for eating and award a sticker to whomever tried the casserole of the day. I encouraged other children to describe how great a food tasted while ignoring Mitchell and leaving it his choice whether he ate to avoid a power struggle.

In an attempt to find the right incentive to encourage Mitchell to eat, I enlisted Santa Claus's aid. Mitchell did like pizza but wouldn't eat our lasagna or spaghetti. One day near Christmas, we had spaghetti. Figuring he would like spaghetti if he would taste it, I told him Santa Clause loved spaghetti and had a co-worker, posing as Santa, talk to Mitchell on the phone. Santa suggested he eat the spaghetti because it was his favorite. It didn't work. So much for the power of "Ho Ho" as Mitchell would call him. Mitchell continued to be disappointed on the days he didn't like anything we served, but his disappointment was not incentive enough to entice him to try anything new.

One day, Mitchell chose not to eat anything at our lunchtime. Knowing Mitchell loved to tease and be teased, I thought I'd try that approach. I dipped his spoon into some chicken noodle soup and asked Mitchell to touch the spoon to his tongue. I thought if he got just a little taste of the broth he might find he liked it, This worked for about three months. Mitchell made a game out of it. He would ask me to watch as he daringly touched the spoon to his tongue. He played this out for my attention, which I lavishly gave so he would participate in this taste-developing game. The other kids began to play the game, too which helped reinforce Mitchell's participation. I thought it really was going to work. Then one day, Mitchell asked in a sad, quiet, voice, "Why do you make me taste that yucky food all the time?" I tried initiating the game a couple more times after that but Mitchell began looking at the food with fear. I knew it was time to stop playing that game. He viewed it as punishment and still wasn't eating.

One day our lunch consisted of meat loaf, mashed potatoes, gravy, green beans, and peaches. Mitchell doesn't eat any of those foods. He asked if we were having bread. I answered, "No." Then he anxiously asked if we were having ice cream for dessert. Again I had to answer, "No." He looked as if he might cry. I stooped beside him, put my arm around his shoulders and explained that this is why I always encourage him to try new foods so he could learn to like them and wouldn't need to be hungry. I asked if he would like to try something that day. He looked toward his lap and just shook his head. I said, "If you change your mind, let me know." Of course, he didn't. Later when we were washing hands for snack Mitchell asked me what we were having to eat. I answered, "Cereal." He smiled and darted to our classroom, but stopped quickly when he saw the kind of cereal and wailed, "I don't like that kind!" He seemed destitute. As tears flooded his anguished face, I encouraged him again to try some, and this was the only time he ever did. He found he sort of liked Kix. He gobbled down three bowls of it. Knowing he tried a new food, at least once, gave me hope. I went back to the drawing board.

I talked to the school psychologist, read everything I could get my hands on, and talked to the school nutritionist who suggested we give him something special to eat on the days he doesn't like our food. I agreed I didn't want him going hungry all day but thought that alternative food also defeated our purpose. It offered him absolutely no incentive to try new foods, which is important for his health and development. I knew his mom and grandma just gave him what they have learned he will eat and didn't encourage him to try anything new. I didn't want to follow that poor example at school. We all drew a blank. Then it came time for our parent-teacher conferences. We always encourage parent volunteers in our school. I thought I would invite Mitchell's mom and grandma to come to our school and hang out in the kitchen. I planned to tell Mitchell that they were teaching our cooks how to prepare his favorite foods. Mitchell's mom agreed and even told Mitchell. He arrived at school the next day excitedly telling me that Mom and Grandma are coming to "show the cooks how to cook!" I was thrilled! I thought maybe I had found a way to get this kid to eat a bigger variety of foods at school, which would transfer to home. Well, the best-laid plans often don't work and this was no exception. His mom and grandma never came, despite several reminder notes. It may not have worked anyhow, but it would have been interesting to see if it would. Now we'll never know.

Mitchell never did expand his eating choices for long term better health. Good nutrition is vital to one's well-being. An interesting study took place in the Central Alternative School in Appleton, Wisconsin. It reports, "The school used to be out of control. Kids packed weapons. Discipline problems swamped the principal's office. But in 1997, a private group called Natural Ovens began a healthy lunch program. Fast-food burgers, fries and burritos gave way to fresh salads, meats prepared with old-fashioned recipes, and whole grain bread. Fresh fruits were added to the menu. Good drinking water arrived. Vending machines were removed. As reported in a newsletter called Pure Facts, "Grades are up, truancy is no longer a problem, arguments are rare, and teachers are able to spend their time teaching. Drop outs, students expelled, students discovered to be using drugs, carrying weapons, committing suicide – every category has come up ZERO. Every year."

Poor diets also lead, or at the very least, add to other maladies. It seems to me that attention deficit disorder (ADHD) was a nonexistent malady before all the fast-foods and processed foods came into abundance and children's lives became consumed with sedentary activities. It is amazing how many children are being medicated for ADHD when most would respond to an adjustment of their diet and physical activity to eliminate the problem. That would be better than putting a band-aid on the problem with unnecessary medication. By the year 2000, over six million American children were prescribed some type of psychotropic drug for ADHD. The American Academy of Pediatrics, in 1998, reported that 10% of all American children ages 6-14 were taking Ritalin, and 1% of all children ages one-five! Statistics show that children on Ritalin and like drugs are far more likely to abuse drugs as a teen and adult. Statistics also show that Ritalin-taking children are more likely to develop serious side-effects as adults, including multiple sclerosis. The Brooklyn National Laboratory studied Ritalin with PET scans of the brain and found it caused a 20-30% decrease in blood flow to the brain. The brain atrophy resulting from long use may be permanent! Cox News Service reported that "All branches of the armed forces reject potential enlistees who use, or used, Ritalin..... even if they no longer take the medication." We must think of long-term effects and how that will affect the child's future. The 50th edition of the Physician's Desk Reference states, "the mode of action is not completely understood....... Ritalin should not be used in children.......since safety and efficacy have not been established." So why do doctors prescribe this? The International Journal of Addictions listed over 100 adverse effects of Ritalin. This can't be good.

A colleague told me about a child in her class with ADHD. She said the mom called to report she had forgotten to give her child his morning dose of Ritalin but he had eaten breakfast — Froot Loops and soda! That child was off the walls! What are they thinking? You really are "what you eat." Artificially colored and sweetened foods are toxic and produce negative side effects. Change that diet! It could keep children off the "chemical strait jacket" (Ritalin) and they'll just plain feel better.

In the book, Born To Buy: The Commercialized Child, Juliet Schor states that, "We will find that toxins, which are proliferating in our food, buildings and environments, not only cause cancer and other health problems but also are linked to growing rates of ADHD, learning disabilities, behavior problems, depression and emotional disorders." Recent news from a Japanese study that rats fed pesticides develop aggressive behavior is very troubling. The effects of junk food are more varied than currently believed. They cause not only weight gain, but also emotional problems such as depressions, anxiety, boredom and impulsive behavior.

The University of Maryland's ADHD Program states that "Treatment for many young children with Attention Deficit/Hyperactivity Disorder should also include treatment for their parents. Parents of children with the condition are 24 times more likely to have the disorder themselves, as compared with the parents of children without ADHD. The study also showed that, when ADHD preschoolers also suffer from other serious behavioral problems, the parents are two to five times more likely to suffer from a wide range of mental health problems, including depression, anxiety and drug addictions." This doesn't surprise me. They follow the same diet and have modeled the same behavior patterns.

It has been suggested that dietary change, such as eliminating sugar, should be one of the first interventions. Also address any food allergies in you child. Correct any nutrient deficiencies, such as, lack of Mg, B6, and certain essential fatty acids. And see a chiropractor. Nerve disturbances in the spine directly affects brain function. This influences not only motor function (hyperactivity disorders) but thought, perception, reaction and other parameters of human behavior. Processing of environmental stimuli is how we express ourselves in every way. We experience our universe through our nervous systems. Caring for it with every tool available is critical. Polluting it with chemicals, thoughts, words, and actions decays our very being. But statistics indicate that parents choose to have their child take a potentially damaging pill as a seemingly quick and easy fix. This saddens me. I have seen the quote: "Every child is born with endless potential. How every child achieves it is up to us." How can we help a child achieve his/her fullest potential when he/she is drugged?

Some of the children who enter our program have never before seen a "full" meal or sat at a table to eat and/or used proper utensils to eat. To them, meal time has been thrown on a paper plate and consumed with fingers while sitting in front of the television set. This conditions a child for mindless eating, among other things. Mealtime is an important family tradition which we need to get back to for many reasons, including healthy food choices.

Proper nutrition is imperative for everyone but especially children. If they don't develop a taste for a variety of foods when they are young, chances are, they never will. It's no wonder our society has a crisis of obesity among young children. They've not been offered nutritional, healthy food choices at an early age. I know both parents need to work these days to make ends meet and sacrifices need to be made, but offering children an apple as a snack instead of an apple Pop Tart is an easy alternative. Offering milk or 100% juice instead of soda makes financial and nutritional sense. Junk food isn't cheap and neither are all the maladies that accompany a diet overindulgent in it. We have definitely become a society which lives to eat - not eats to live.

Food, too often, fills voids in children's lives left by parents who put his/ her own agenda ahead of their children's. Food becomes a child's comfort, security and feeling of being loved and indulged. It is also indicative of today's "feel good" society. If it feels good at the moment, do it and don't worry about the consequences.

We need to return to the days when fresh fruits and vegetables were put into the grocery cart first and foremost and, if a bag of chips were bought, they had to last two weeks. They were to be a snack not a meal. Soda is not a necessity. It's an expensive highly addictive, sugary rush. This addiction is a hard habit to break, but it's worth it, for everyone.

You can lead a child to food but you can't make him eat. But he can't eat what isn't there. So keep those unhealthy food choices at the grocery store. Teach them how to make lifelong good food choices. Chef Bobo's secret: cooking from scratch, trimming portion sizes and substituting healthier versions of kids' high-fat, preservative-laden faves. Doing this, he states, will "satisfy even the pickiest of eaters." If his book would have been around then, I would have tried it. Next time.......Next Mitchell!

Chapter Twenty-three

Abby

Abby taught me .... children are inventive storytellers.

Abby was a quiet child who often needed extra attention. For instance when the rest of the children would line up, Abby would lay on the beanbag and often looked very sad and dejected. After receiving her fill of hugs, she would promptly join the group. I asked her mom about this. She said she'd ask Abby why she was doing these things. When questioned, Abby made up a story about another child in the class picking on her. I found that unlikely since Abby's behavior started long before the other child even started in our class. I mentioned this to the mom, who became upset because she thought her child was a liar. I assured her that Abby did not intentionally lie

I explained children at this age are often confused by fantasy and reality. I further explained that when preschoolers are questioned and they really don't know the answer yet, they make up what they think is an acceptable answer. When we demand an explanation at this age we are forcing them to become creative storytellers. If you ask a child, "Why did you hit Johnny?" What could she possibly tell you that would be an acceptable justification for her actions? If she answers "because he took my toy" are you going to say, "Oh, o.k. then. Yea, hit him!" No, and a child probably knows that, so she knows she has to make up a doosie of a story!

The truth is, young children don't know why they hit. Impulsive little ones react before they think. It's what they do because it's what they're developmentally ready to do. One reason children have parents/caregivers is to prevent the consequences of their impulsivity. Even though a child has been told 100 times to stay on the sidewalk, chances are, she will dart out on the road to chase a ball that has gotten away from her; or touch a hot pan after being warned of the chance of injury if one does; or the classic, stick one's tongue on a flagpole in Minnesota in January. After one of these incidences, it is common for a child to make a story about why she felt compelled to do it. Sometimes the child can come up with a seemingly, reasonable explanation and sometimes, she finds a scapegoat and tattles.

Oh tattling! Children usually tattle for two reasons. One is to clarify the rules in order to feel safe and secure. It would be likened to you going on your first white water rafting ride and you were a little unsettled. The rafting guide goes over the instructions rather quickly. Since you want to make sure you've got it right, you'd most likely check with your neighboring rafter to assure yourself that you heard and followed through correctly. If you saw someone else being jacketed incorrectly you may point this out to the guide; not with the intent of getting that other guy in trouble but to make sure you are properly jacketed. This reassurance would make you feel more secure.

The second reason for tattling is to manipulate with the intent of getting someone else in trouble. This kind of kid likes control and/or wants to divert attention away from his/her wrongdoing. This details a reason to understand that children are good storytellers. She may be just trying to test how well she has developed her acting and storytelling ability. The first time my brother cut my hair, I was probably about five years old. I sat back and enjoyed the sweet revenge of seeing him punished for his amateur barber deeds. When I was mad at him because he wouldn't let a «girl» be on his team, I told him I liked how he cut my hair before and asked if he would cut it again. I figured he'd be punished again. Imagine my surprise when Mom grounded both of us. My brother for cutting my hair and me for letting him. Whoops! It backfired! This time my brother's punishment was bitter sweet for him because he enjoyed the revenge of seeing me endure punishment too. I don't think I ever tried to get him into trouble again.

He didn't rest until he got me back, though. One time he and his friend reluctantly permitted me to play with them, probably after I whined enough and threatened to tell Mom if he wouldn't let me play. When he suggested I could be the animal and he and Tim would be the trappers, I felt honored that he was allowing me to be the all important animal. Well, that honor turned to pain as I stepped into the first trap. I learned in the snap of a second that they used real traps and had set it for real. And it really hurt! I didn't have to tattle on him for that one. When my blood curdling screams caused my mom to come running, she saw my brother and his friend frantically trying to open the trap so I could free my foot. Yea, they got grounded, and I got ice for my ankle.

But I digress. Remember too, it's likely that kids at this age honestly get information bungled. I always laugh when I remember the time I explained to my group of students that I was going to be absent for a couple of days to go on a little vacation in celebration of my tenth wedding anniversary. Since I was a seasoned teacher of preschoolers, I knew just how to explain it to them so they would understand perfectly, right? Apparently not! When I returned, a few parents congratulated me on my recent nuptials. One mom reported that her son told her that I was getting married for the tenth time! She didn't know whether to congratulate me or feel sorry for me! The best was when one girl told her mom I was marrying ten men. Sometimes kids get information bungled on purpose. There was a mom who questioned me about her son's reports of us spending the day jumping off the roof onto a parachute. We had played with the parachute that day but there was definitely no jumping. We couldn't. Our ripcords were missing! Just kidding! You have to admire this kids imagination! Another child told me that his mom was pregnant and gave me details of her doctors visits and what sex the baby was and everything. Boy, was I ever embarrassed when I congratulated the mom only to find out she wasn't pregnant at all. In fact, she had her tubes tied after her last baby was born. Yet another reminder to not believe everything a child says. Sometimes you know immediately that a child is reporting inaccurately. I had a kid tell me that he had a giraffe in his back yard and it eats bananas. One child told me he went to Disney World "last night." Another child told me he went on a rocket to McDonalds. When I asked what she ate for breakfast, one child answered, "Glass and worms and dirt." This year a boy told me that all the Easter Bunny brought him was a basketfull of mayonnaise! Just the other day an angry and concerned Dad called me stating he wasn't going to send his daughter to school because when she got home yesterday, she reported to him that I "pulled her out of lunch and checked her head then made her stay on the playground the whole rest of the day." He defended his daughter by saying he believes her and knows she isn't a liar. I think he understood about children's stories by the end of our conversation.

Of course some reports mirror the life a child has to lead. For example, one boy proudly announced that he's been in jail three times. Of course, this is the same boy who was excited because he visited his Dad the previous night. Unfortunately it was through the window at the jail.

I love how kids figure out how life works. A group of children were playing in a sensory table that was filled with styrofoam peanuts. One girl was explaining to the rest that "when you get old your hair gets white then you die." (That day after school, I made an appointment with my hair dresser to have my hair colored.) A boy involved in that discussion said, "My Dad died last night." I had seen his Dad just that morning or I may have been alarmed.

During snack one day, a boy proudly announced to a girl that his grandma could whoop her grandma! My aide and I looked at each other and slightly nodded. We had dibs on the boy's grandma. Just kidding! I wondered if the grandma would have been proud that her grandson holds her in this regard!

There is nothing more humbling than having a child repeat something you've said, especially if the time or place isn't appropriate. We took one of my former students to a little play one summer. The character, Grandpa Cratchet, explained to the audience that Grandma kept hiding his teeth, and asked what he should do with Grandma. This little girl in our company stood straight up and enthusiastically shouted, "Beat her! Beat her!" I wanted to curl up smaller than an ant as everyone turned to look at us. I was hoping that her fair blonde hair differing from the dark hair of both my husband and me would clue people to the fact that this isn't our child. But just in case, I think I did mumble, "She's not our child." Yea, I'm sure everyone believed that old line.

The play, Into the Wood, has a great song titled, "Children Will Listen." Some of the lyrics are: "Careful the things you say, children will listen. Careful before you say, "listen to me!" Children will listen. Careful the tale you tell, that is the spell. Children will listen. What can you say that no matter how slight won't be misunderstood? Careful what you say, children will listen. Careful what you do, children will see and learn. Children may not obey, but children will listen." Those lyrics sure ring true. And remember what you say and do may be repeated, embellished or misquoted, out of the mouths of babes!

Chapter Twenty-Four

Hannah

Hannah taught me- What is important to a child may not seem important to an adult and visa versa.

I took Hannah to a store the other day and was reminded of how long she takes to choose her purchases. It was an accessory store and I think she studied every single barrette and trinket on display. I noticed her face as she focused on her task. Her studious expression depicted the seriousness of her mission from which she couldn't be distracted. She barely acknowledged her brothers comments. This important decision took her approximately 40 minutes to finalize. The same thing occurred when I had taken her to a fabric store for the first time. It was old hat to me but she was thrilled with the varied selection of colors and textures and prints. It was so cute. That trip took three times longer than if I had gone myself but it sure wouldn't have been as memorable.

Hannah's lengthy, focused undertaking reminded me what was very important to her. For her, this was not a decision to be made lightly. Since we adults have to make endless decision every day- sometimes it feels like every minute- we forget that these seemingly petty decisions are a big deal to a child. If rushed, they become very anxious. They haven't yet learned to trust their instincts or judgment. It takes more time for them to process all information than it does for an adult. We have more practice. Nathaniel Branden, author, writes, "Having self-esteem entails trust in one's own mind." Children need these opportunities to develop the confidence that is crucial in life.

It's easy for adults to view shopping as just shopping and playing as just playing. What we need to remember is that each offers opportunities for children to develop needed skills. When children are playing they are learning to work out issues. This shouldn't be taken lightly and dismissed as unimportant. Often a child's play cannot be ended quickly and effortlessly. The child may have had a particular outfit in mind and it is important to her to see her intent carried through. Children need time to dress a doll in a manner in which the child feels is proper and complete. We need to keep in mind this isn't trivial- this is important stuff to a child. Rushing the process can be devastating to a child. This could be likened to an adult missing the last 10 minutes of a movie or a tied hockey game. It's frustrating. You had planned to watch it to the end. You had an idea how it was going to end but had a desire to see it through. Then, all of a sudden, without warning, you are instructed to finish watching, now! This is what it can feel like to a child to require them to stop their play before they are ready.

It is so important to give children, at least, a two minute advance warning that their play time is ending. It was apparent, early on, that Hannah needed much more than two minutes to wrap up her current course of action. This is typical of many children. For those, it is wise to start warning that playtime is ending, at least, 20 minutes ahead of time. Subsequent warnings at four or five minutes intervals is helpful in facilitating a smooth transition. This is also a helpful technique because it helps teach children to manage their time and thoughts.

I get very frustrated in my classroom because I see how the restraints of time negatively affect the children. Frequently, we have to stop one activity to prepare for another because of a schedule. It is important for children to learn there is structure and order in their life but it's a shame their creativity and growth are often restricted because of an external clock that fits someone else's agenda.

Many other seemingly trivial rituals can mean all the difference to a child. Zoe was the middle child of a single-parent home. She was long and lean and very intelligent. She didn't play much with her peers but instead would seek out adults in the room with whom to interact. She loved just hanging around the adults and loved even more to be held and cuddled.

As every preschool teacher knows, one can never come in from recess without a pocketful of dandelions. I never realized that those hearty little yellow weeds grow from early March to late November. Zoe was a serious dandelion picker. It isn't important for me to fill my pockets with these but it was an important ritual of Zoe's to present me with every dandelion she could possibly find on our playground. It became routine to rid my pockets of dried dandelions at the end of each school day. I admit I actually like dandelions but enough is enough! However in the eyes of a child, a teacher can never have enough yellow symbols of pure appreciation, devotion and love. They are an important offering to a child. A good preschool teacher will never loose one's appreciation of the symbol these weeds represent. I'm sure some left-over seeds from those discarded weeds end up at my home and multiply passionately. As I seemingly have more and more each Spring, I remind myself the importance of the first flower a child gives to the adult they admire. Then I don't mind them so much as I endlessly spray them with Round-Up.

Another important offering came from Zoe one year for Christmas, when she proudly presented me with a gift. It was apparent she had wrapped it herself (my favorite kind!) and she had created a card to accompany the gift. I made a big fuss over the whole presentation and the thought behind it. When I unwrapped the gift, I saw it was a watch. Knowing the family had a very limited income, I became nervous about accepting such a gift and even found myself wondering where Zoe got this watch and if it were even meant for me. My apprehension all ended when I realized it was an old watch. Her eyes gleamed as she asked me to put it on. It was only after it was on my wrist that I discovered it didn't even work anymore. She had given me a broken watch and was as pleased as if she had given me a brand new Rolex. And it pleased me more than any expensive gift ever could.

Of course, I had to continue to make a big fuss over this thoughtful gift. When we returned from Christmas vacation, I had almost forgotten about the watch, which I had hung in my closet. One of the first things Zoe did upon returning was ask if I was wearing the watch. I thanked her for reminding me and explained that I had just washed my hands and hadn't put it back on yet. I immediately adorned my wrist with her valued present. She was thrilled and asked me several times that day what time it was or looked to see that I was still wearing it. Each time her smile was as big as the the face on Big Ben. After that, I wore that broken watch every single day for the rest of the school year. She made a habit of looking for it and would reassuringly smile at the sight of it, every time. It became one of the best presents I'd ever received in my life. It kept giving day after day after day. What started out to be very important to her became very important to me as well. Thank you, Zoe.

Hannah gave me such an offering, too in the form of a bracelet. I wasn't sure when it might be appropriate to wear this plastic, multi-colored, beaded beauty, but I wanted her to know I appreciated her efforts and thoughtfulness. I decided to hang it from the rear-view mirror in my car. The first time she saw it hanging there was so cute. She asked, in disbelief, "Is that my bracelet?" I said, "Yes, and isn't is beautiful!" It meant a lot to her that I displayed it where all could see.

If you have a child in your life, chances are, you have artwork on your refrigerator. It is so important to a child to have their crafts displayed proudly. That's better than hanging a sign that reads, 'I love you and you are special." No one even has to stop to make a fuss over their artwork. Just knowing you took the time to post it, means so much to them. There's a saying, "If God had a refrigerator, your picture would be on it." Makes you feel good to hear and know that, doesn't it? That's how a child feels when seeing her picture on the refrigerator of one who cares. Not much effort on your part but an important exhibition to a child.

On the other hand, the tasks we prioritize are quite unimportant to a child. The same day as the accessory purchase, I knew we needed to get back to the house because we had flour all over the floor from making play dough and I had told the kids we would make a cake for their mom's birthday. It was also very close to dinnertime. That all adds up to stress, restrictions and an annoying ticking clock to an adult. The kids couldn't have cared less. None of that meets their needs and they aren't even capable of understanding the steps all these chores require. They're just along for the ride, so to speak.

It's the same as when you know you need to get somewhere at a certain time and the kids just won't get those shoes on. They aren't, believe it not, just acting totally unconcerned, they are totally unconcerned. Okay, you finally get them outside. Now we can go directly to the car. Right? Wrong! They are throwing snow in the air and taking a "snow shower." How could they possibly be engaging in this nonsensical activity when we need to get going? And why doesn't it move them along when we remind them that, "We're going to be late!" Even informing them to hurry because, "It's cold out here!" doesn't help get them in the warm car any quicker either. They're just carefree. I think the Power of Now book could have been written by a child because they really are the ones who understand and practice the power of the present.

Richard Carlson writes in his book, Stop Thinking Start Living, about ways for an adult to be happy. Some of us have gotten so far removed from it that we have to learn how to be happy. He also realizes that children don't need to be taught how to be happy; in fact we can learn from them. He states: "Happy people understand, either instinctual or because they have been taught, that the name of the game is to enjoy life rather than to think about it. Happy people are so immersed in the process of life, absorbed in what they are doing at the moment, that they rarely stop to analyze how they are doing. If you want to verify this concept first-hand, spend some time watching a roomful of preschool children. The reason they're having such a good time is because all of their energy is directed towards enjoyment. They are immersed in whatever they are doing; they aren't keeping score." Kids are blasé about whether lunch is at 12:00 or 1:00. It doesn't stress them out. All they know is they eat when they are hungry. Who cares what a clock indicates? They are indifferent to our goals of scrubbing the floors or getting the laundry done. So when we stress about these chores and display this to children, they feel the apprehension but can't understand the urgency. All they want is for an adult to give them some attention and to feel their needs are respected and met. Nathaniel Branden states, "When your children are talking, look at them and listen while they are speaking. Don't cut them off or finish sentences for them. Don't unnecessarily correct them or do other work when they are talking to you. They can sense our impatience or lack of interest." Children are egotistical and self-absorbed and they can't help it. It's just where they're at developmentally. It would be as unfair to expect them to be anything else; just as it would be unfair to ask them to balance your checkbook or drive the car. They can't be expected to understand the importance of the pressures adults face. And they shouldn't be. They should just be allowed to be kids.

The next time I want to hurry a child along I'll ask myself what I'm missing at that moment. Is my schedule really that important or is it more important to I see how the gift of time is enjoyed by a child? Empathize with the need of a child to live in the moment. Value the process. That is important to both a child and an adult. Enjoy it together.

Chapter Twenty-five

Cloe

Cloe taught me......................Prepare children for the inevitable part of life - death.

When my mother-in-law died, all her children, grandchildren, and some great grandchildren came to the funeral home, of course. On the evening of the viewing, one of her grandsons came with his daughter. This 10 year old stood at the opposite end of the room from the coffin, looking quite frightened. After about five minutes, an older cousin of hers asked if she wanted to go see Grandma. Cloe nodded an almost undetectable yes.

It was obvious that Cloe wasn't sure about what she was going to see, or how she was going to feel, once at the casket. She approached slowly and cautiously, with a sad, fearful expression on her downward focused face. Her hand was holding that of her cousin, who was leading the way. Sensing her obvious trepidation, I decided I should accompany them to the casket. Someone else came in at that moment who immediately engaged me in conversation.

A short time later I noticed, amid all the sympathy wishers, Cloe sitting in the chair, all by herself, closest to the casket. Her posture was very stiff and her head was turned away from the casket but her eyes were stretched toward the casket. I went over and sat beside her. I did the usual, "Hi! How are you?" She looked down and nodded and spoke a quiet, "Okay." I asked, "How are you feeling about all this?" She answered, "I don't know. I guess, sort'a sad." I said, "Well, you're doing okay then because this is sad. It's normal to feel sad and sometimes, it's okay to feel sad." We sat quietly for a couple minutes then I asked, "Have you ever been to a funeral before?" She said, "No." I said, "Is it anything like you expected?" She said, "No." I asked, "Do you want to tell me in what ways it is different?" She said, "Well, I thought that (as she motioned to the casket) would be lower to the ground." I said, "That might make it harder for adults to see, huh?" She said, "Yeah." I continued, "But it would make it easier for you to see, wouldn't it?" She answered as she studied the room, "Yea, maybe." Just then one of her cousins came to us and invited Cloe to play in the basement with the other kids. She looked at me for my reaction. I said, "You go play if you want to." She said, "I kinda feel too sad to play. I guess it's alright that they play 'cause they're littler and maybe they don't know how sad this is." I said, "Yea, they'll understand when they get big like you." I could tell she had a lot more on her mind, so I continued asking questions. I asked, "What else is different?" She said, "I didn't think Grandma would have so much make-up on. Why does she have so much make-up on?" I answered honestly, " I don't know why. But I think she does too." Then I followed her lead as she stood and stepped to the casket. She touched the white blanket that draped the sides of the casket and asked, "Do they fold this in when they close the lid?" I said, "I'm not sure but I bet they do. That's a good question. Do you want me to go ask the man who runs the funeral home?" She looked at me with a panic in her eyes and quickly answered, "No!" as she lunged toward me. I said, "No problem. I won't." as I touched her shoulder. She looked around and asked, "Will they cover her with this blanket when they bury her?" Now I wasn't sure how to answer this question to this inquisitive little mind. I didn't know how much she knew or how much information she could handle but I said, "Well, Grandma isn't going to be buried in this casket. She wanted to be cremated." I was waiting for Cloe to ask me what cremated meant. I wasn't sure how I was going to explain that to her because I wasn't sure what she was ready to hear. Just then another cousin came to us. We had some idle chit-chat then she told Cloe her dress was pretty and pointed out it was the same color as the skirt around the bottom of the casket. Cloe said stoically, "I like purple. It's my favorite." As soon as this cousin left, Cloe asked, "Will she sleep in here tonight?" I explained that she will lay there tonight and tomorrow morning. We will come back tomorrow for services; which is like a church service, then she will go to a special place where they cremate people and they will put her ashes in a beautiful urn. I asked, "Do you know what an urn is?" She said, "Yea, it's like a vase with a lid on it." I said, "Wow are you smart. That's a good description and you're exactly right." Then she asked, "What will they do with Grandma's jewelry?" I said, "The family has instructed the funeral people to put it in the urn with her ashes. Then we are going to have her ashes buried in the cemetery beside Grandpa." She looked very sad and after a long pause said, "I want to come here tomorrow but Daddy said I have to go to school." I said, "It would probably be good if you went to school tomorrow because it's only your second day back this Fall and you'll have a lot to do." She said, "But I'll just be sad and won't be able to concentrate, anyhow and I'll probably even cry." I said, "Does Daddy know how important it is to you to come here tomorrow?" She said, "I told him!" I said, "Well, I'm sure Daddy feels it would be best for you right now to go to school." She looked down at the floor and said, "But I just want to come." I said, "Could you ask Daddy to bring a picture of you with him tomorrow and I'll tuck it in with Grandma and that way you can be with her tomorrow." She brightened a bit and said, "Yea.! That would be good." Then I looked at the flower arrangement on the casket and said, "And see this purple iris right here?" She said, "Yea." I said, "I'll pull this out of here tomorrow and send it home with Daddy for you." She asked, "Does everyone get to take home a flower?" I said, "No, but I think it's pretty important that you have this flower." She smiled and gave me a hug.

As she left that evening with her dad, I told him that this had been a little hard on Cloe and that she may have a lot more questions for him and may have difficulty falling asleep. I suggested that he let her fall asleep in his arms tonight and be very patient with her because this was really an emotional experience for her.

After services the next day, I gathered that purple flower and a few others, to create a bouquet for Cloe. I made absolutely certain that it made it to her dad's car. I hope it helped.

I recently attended a seminar in Pittsburgh presented by Daniel Opalewski about death and dying. One of the key points he stressed is that it's okay to take young children to a funeral home and in fact, a good thing. But they need to be prepared for what they are going to see. He specifically advised to describe how the deceased may not look the same and go into detail what they may look like, including make-up. He stated that thousands of school age children die each year. In addition, thousands more experience the death of a parent or grandparent. We need to be proactive in the handling of a crisis. We can not fix a tragedy, but when handled properly, we can grow from it. Daniel explained, "When communicating with a child, proximity is very important. The closer you are to the child, the more effective the communication." He advised, "Sit in the same type of chair as the child, no desk or table in between. Sit so you are at eye level. Introduce touch. A gentle touch with a finger or hand on the forearm is very calming. Don't touch if the child is agitated. Use active listening - repeat questions or concerns. Keep your tone of voice warm and personal. When we model warmth and caring, people are more inclined to treat us with respect."

Even if a child has been to a funeral home before, prepare them each time according to the situation and the level at which the child is at developmentally. One of my sister's recounted her experiences of funerals as a child. She remembers that when she attended the funeral of our grandparents, the children were playing carefree in the basement. They were chastised for this seemingly lack of disrespect. Then she remembers attending the funeral home to view our youngest sibling, who died when he was nine months old. She said the thing that stuck out the most was how small the coffin was. She thought it would be a full-sized coffin as she had experienced twice before in the deaths of adult members of our extended family. Every experience is different and the child needs to be prepared for that.

The same guidelines apply if you take children into a hospital room of a very sick or hurt loved one. They need advance notice of what they are going to see. They need to know they are going to hear beeps and buzzers and they are going to see tubes and lights and a lot of people in white clothes and masks. They are going to smell those distinctive hospital smells. The loved one may feel hot or cold. They may be able to talk or not talk. They may open their eyes or not open their eyes. Whatever the case may be. Prepare them.

I learned through my mother-in-laws passing from Hospice, that the hearing is the last sense to go when someone is dying. So it's important to encourage a child or anyone to talk or sing to their loved one, right up to the end, if they are comfortable doing that. I take it even farther - I believe they can continue to hear you even after their spirit leaves their body. I encourage my god kids to speak to their deceased grandfathers all the time. They seem to take comfort in doing this. I'm sure their grandfathers do too. But if a child isn't ready to do this, it's important to not force them.

I recently heard the theory that people who learn to cope well with loss, live longer than those who don't. I'm not sure how that was determined but it makes sense. Knowing this reinforces that helping a child experience this inevitable part of life, is an important life lesson for children which they will draw upon many times the rest of their lives.

Young children aren't able to discern between fantasy and reality. They aren't able to understand that when a person dies, they are dead forever. Be careful not to explain that a dead person is "just sleeping." When that person is never seen again, the child will fear that when someone sleeps, they disappear. Be honest. Tell the child the person's body stopped performing all the necessary functions to support life. Explain that the person they see lying the in the casket is not going to come back to life. It's a difficult reality but it is best dealt with honestly and without vague analogies. Do this before ever entering a funeral home. This will help prepare them to understand a funeral is a marker to lay it to rest, forever.

Chapter Twenty-six

Noah

Noah taught me......I can hear, see, touch and smell love.

My godson, Noah, spent eight days at the beach with his parents and sister. Upon their return, Noah talked to me for an hour on the phone. That's right! I had an hour-long conversation with a five-year-old on the phone. There were no lulls in the exchange, no awkward moments, no wondering what we were going to talk about next. Just one full hour of hearing his wonderful voice and thoughts. It occurred to me after that precious hour that I heard love. And it's like no other sound. It's indescribable. With his words, he told me about the beach and the grass that's growing behind the cottage and giants and lobster and boogies and anything else that came to his formative mind. He shared his five-year-old infinite wisdom with me. Such as the wonderment of figuring out that when the sun goes behind the clouds it's cloudy, and when it comes out, it's sunny. It's just that simple. That's how Noah sees all of life. So practical but magical. I'm glad Noah doesn't let me forget that simple logic just because I have aged.

He also enlightened me as to how lobster meat gets into the lobster! He explained that the waiter splits the lobster and puts the food inside then closes it up and cooks it and gives it to you so you can split it open and get the food out. He said, "and there's green stuff in there that looks like salad but it's not, and the waiter put that in there, too." In case you ever wondered how that's done, that's how it's done in the mind of a five-year-old.

His voice sounds so good to me. With his limited vocabulary, I heard words, but with his soul, I heard love. And of course, his laugh is lovingly contagious. His laugh is the sound of love. His voice is the sound of love. No matter what he says, when I hear Noah, I hear love.

I discovered I can see love the day I met the kids at their swimming lessons. As I approached the building, I could see Noah through the glass doors. He was mundanely looking around at other kids hurrying by in their dripping swimsuits. Then the magical moment of seeing love appeared. Noah looked through the doors, and upon seeing me approaching, instantly flashed a smile that truly covered his entire face. It was a beautiful sight. It was a vision of love. With that smile, I could see the love in Noah and the love coming out of Noah toward me. Thanks Noah, for letting me see love. I swear a blind person would be able to see all the love that radiates from you.

Chapter 10 on how beautiful Noah makes my hands feel explains how I can touch love but that's only part of it. Ever since Noah was little he had a way of cuddling so snugly into me, that I thought we'd need surgery to remove him. Of course, I would never opt to have that surgery! I can't imagine how lonely it must feel to not get a hug when needed. Research states that people can live without sight, smell, or hearing, and with very little food, but can't survive without being touched. Its power to connect humans is unmatched. Judy Rigby, a registered practitioner from North London, through The Blue Lotus Rising recently published "The Importance Of Touch." She wrote: "Psychologists have demonstrated that our perception of how much and how we are touched relates to how we value ourselves." Thirteenth century historian Salimbene described an experiment made by the German Emperor Frederick II, who wanted to know which language children would speak if raised in isolation. The result was that they all died. "They could not live without petting. Nor can anyone else. Untouched adults may not die physically, but life will not be experienced to the full."

Nathaniel Branden writes, "Long before a child can understand words, he understands touch. Declarations of love without touch are unconvincing and hollow. Hugging and kissing your child and holding his hand are very basic and important ways of expressing love, comfort, support and nurturing. Through touch we send sensory stimulation that helps the child's brain develop." Deprivation syndromes actually exist from the lack of touch. Bernadette Murgor published in the Standard that "The effects of touch deprivation are classified as immunological, physiological, and behavioral. Lack of touch may result in a tendency to avoid social contact, to be hyper-aggressive and to exhibit anger and depression symptoms."

I always feel badly when I see a dog tethered to a chain outside the home of the ones to whom he and is entrusted to. I'm sure he received hugs as a puppy and now is discarded because he got too big or was too destructive or because the baby was born. He has to crave that hug. What a sad, lonely existence. The true meaning of being lonely, according to Iyanla Vanzant, is when we "seek and crave or lust after the very thing we believe we cannot have." I'm sure that dog would be happy if the owner would have saved just one of the hugs he received so lavishly as a puppy. I wonder if the owner is aware that touch is said to heighten the efficacy of the immune system in animals. It also slows heart rate and decreases blood pressure in humans. Touching is mutually beneficial.

Sometimes the children in my class need only a hug. Not a lecture or discipline or time out- just a hug. Bernadette Murgor stated that, "We need to be aware of our children's innate needs. Holding, rocking, hugging and cuddling a child does not constitute "spoiling," but is an instinctual response to a child's primary needs for love, security, and affection, in as much as providing nutrition is necessary to a child's physical well-being." I know that a hug from Noah is crucial to my well-being. Ever wonder why an infant falls asleep so easily when cradled in the arms of a trusted, loved one? It's such a safe, warm, secure place to be. I know many friends who have gone through rough times. It's not what I've said that they remember as much as the hug I provided. I just received an e-mail passing a hug along through the computer. Even those one-dimensional hugs can mean a lot. It isn't the same, of course, but sparks a good memory in our brains.

When people hug they exchange more than human contact. They exchange energy fields. That is one reason why hug therapy is so effective. I believe in the healing power of touch. It can't be a fluke of nature for us to have inherited the instinct to instantly touch something that hurts. Studies have shown that people react more positively to one another if a simple, quick touch is added to their exchange. Waitresses even gain financially from touch. It has been proven that they receive better tips if they touch their patrons. The chiropractic profession is wisely aware of the positive affects of touch. Chiropractor, in Latin, means done by hand. Machines can't replace that personal-healing touch. But nothing compares to the loving touch of Noah. It is how love feels. Noah's touch goes the whole way to my heart.

Now the olfactory part of love....... Noah has always smelled everything so it's fitting that I'm talking about smelling and Noah. He smelled all his food, he smelled his clothes, the dog, his stuffed animals, pillows, wood, bugs, leaves, everything he got his hands on, he smelled. But I smell love every time I bathe Noah. He smells so pure and sweet; warm and gentle; refreshed and pleasant; comfortable and heavenly, and complete. Recently he has gotten into spritzing some of his dad's cologne on his chest after his bath. He claims he smells handsome. He likes that! But I know when he grows to be a handsome man and wears that cologne for real, I'll miss the smell of truitty fruitty shampoo that comes out of a character bottle. On Noah, that is the smell of pure, unadulterated love.

We tend to ignore our senses as we grow. Successful meditation is accomplished by using all one's senses. To enjoy and experience life to the fullest, we need to get in touch with all our primal senses. I thank Noah for enabling me to live fully. He really fills up my senses.

Chapter Twenty-seven

Hannah

Hannah taught me.................My presence is purposeful.

One day in the car, my god daughter told me they had an assignment in school. They had to write four things for which they were thankful and four reasons why they were thankful for each. She said one of the things she wrote she was thankful for was me. As if I wasn't touched enough already, she added, "but I couldn't stop at four reasons why for you. I wrote like seven or eight." Of course the only thing that kept me from crying more than a couple tears of sheer happiness at that time was the fact that I was driving.

A couple weeks after that Hannah started mentioning a play in school about the Indians and Pilgrims that she wanted me to come see. She wasn't sure, at that time, what date the play was on. I told her to let me know as soon as possible so I could get a substitute teacher for my class on that day. Upon learning the date, she called and left a message on my answering machine. It was SO cute. She said, "MaryAnn, you know that play I'm gonna be in, well it's on the 18th. November 18th. Just make sure you get a substitute by then because it's gonna be.....I don't know what time, but it's a play; and it's on the 18th. That's a one and an eight. Eeeigh-teen-th! 18th! Bye. I love you, a lot!" That message is a keeper! Her mom e-mailed me the Tuesday before the play with the times. I gasped when I read it was to be at 9:20 and a second performance at 10:30. I had an important meeting at 9:30! What was I going to do?

I replied to Hannah's mom explaining my scheduling conflict. I think my exact words were, "This sucks!" I really wanted to be there but didn't feel I could get out of this meeting. But determined not to disappoint Hannah (or myself), I thought I might be able to get out of the meeting quickly and make it to the 10:30 show. I asked my supervisor how long she thought the meeting would last. Her guess was about an hour. Then sensing I had a specific intent for asking that question, she quarried, "Why?" I explained about Hannah's play. She understood immediately and said, "Go!" I confirmed, "Are you sure?" It was actually too good to be true! After telling me that she has been in that same conflict in her own life she said she was sure that there was nothing more important than for me to be there for this little girl. I was elated and so appreciative.

I didn't notify Hannah with my change of plans. I thought I'd just surprise her. And it worked out beautifully! I entered the room behind her parents. I saw her smile at her parents and beam upon seeing my unexpected presence. It was great already. Little did I know, the best was yet to come.

Another child's grandmother sat to the left of me. While waiting for the play to begin, she recognized Hannah's dad as an acquaintance and leaned past me to speak to him. She asked him if he had a son or daughter in the play. He didn't hear her correctly as he was being spoken to from the right as well. So, I answered for him. She asked my connection to the family. I explained that Hannah is my god daughter and we spend as much time together as possible. Then the play began. This kindly grandmother whispered, "Which one is his daughter?" I answered, "You can't see her yet but she is dressed as an Indian and is holding a baby. She's the tallest one in the class and she is really beautiful!" When Hannah appeared on stage, her dad leaned past me to boast to the grandma, "That's my daughter. She just happens to be beautiful, isn't she?!" The grandmother and I smiled at each other and she said, "Yes, I've heard that!"

Hannah did a great job and glanced back frequently for approving smiles. After applauding the little actors and actresses, I thought the whole wonderful experience was over. But then, each child who had a family member in the audience read his or her, "What I'm Thankful For" essay. We listened to several children before Hannah. Of course they were sweet and some were funny. Then Hannah stood in front of us and began reading, confidently and articulately, "What I'm Thankful For by Hannah Schwartz. I'm thankful for my babysitter. I have the best babysitter in the whole world." I was crying already. I've never heard such sweet words in my entire life. She continued, "And we are going to stay overnight at her house on November 12th and I'm happy about that. She has been taking care of me since I was a baby and I love her." Noticing I was searching for a tissue to wipe away my happy tears, the grandma gave me one and said, "You are really special in that little girl's life." I said, "And she in mine!" I'm a little embarrassed to admit that I'm not sure what else Hannah said in her essay because I was in a blissful fog.

After the last child read his essay, Hannah worked her way through the crowd to me. She gave me a big hug. As I gratefully hugged her I said, "I am SO proud of you. You did such a good job. And thank you so much for your Thanksgiving words. I'm thankful for you, too. I love you!" Just then her teacher called her back to the group. As she walked toward her classmates she said, "I love you, too." The grandmother who witnessed this exchange said, "I don't know you, but you must be really something for that little girl to stand up there and say all that about you." I said, "She is the one that is really something!" As I was leaving, three other people stopped me and said, "You must be the babysitter." I've never worn a title more proudly. Upon leaving, I thanked her teacher for letting family and friends come to the little production. He asked, "Who are you here with?" I proudly answered, "Hannah Schwartz." He said, "Ah! You're the babysitter. She talks a lot about you."

My feet didn't touch the ground the whole way to my car. What an honor. What a tribute. What a special little girl. How thankful I am to have her unselfish, earnest love expressed privately and publicly to me. I love you, Hannah.

Sometimes I wonder if she hears what I am explaining to her or if she understands and appreciates it. But this indicated she has heard every word and understood the love and caring behind each and every one. We rarely have the opportunity to really identify the moments that define our purpose in life. If we do, it is sometime after the fact and almost as an after note. And sometimes you don't ever know that something you said to a person years or decades ago shaped their life in a positive way. So it is extra special to have someone spell it out as clearly and sincerely as Hannah did in my presence. That is not something everyone will have the pleasure of experiencing in a whole lifetime.

A few quick weeks later, Hannah once again expressed her admiration for me this time in a Christmas book she composed in school. She made her own wrapping paper and presented it to me with other Christmas presents. The book is in a shape of a house. She titled it, <u>Jesus is Born</u> by Hannah Schwartz. First page: "Jesus is Born. Written and Illustrated by Hannah Schwartz. December 22, 2004. Dedicated to My Babysitter Maryann." Okay, I was in tears already. I must explain that each page is adorned with beautiful, colorful pictures that she created. I wish you could see them, I'll just share the rest of the text. "*Christmas is the best time of the year.*

Christmas is when you spend time with your mom and dad. Love is the most precious gift in the world. Love is when you like someone very much. I am going to give the gift of Love by telling my babysitter Maryann that I Love her very much........ I am going to tell her I don't want her to go away. Without her Love, the wold would be miserable. I wish I had more time to do the things I want to do with her. Time is a wonderful gift we can give this Christmas. I want to spend time this Christmas with the person I love, to show her that I Love her....... I know someone that has just one friend and I am going to be her new friend this Christmas. She seems nice. That is what manners my babysitter taught me that her name is Maryann. The gift of friendship is a wondeful thing....... Haunkkah is a time for helping and making latkes because it helps us remember in the past when the Temple of Jerusalem got knocked down. I love the holidays!...........Christmas is when we celebrate the Festival of Lights...........I am going to make this a special Christmas by giving the gifts of time, prayer, Love, and Friendship........ About the Author. Hannah Schwartz. I am 8 years old. I am in 2ⁿᵈ grade at Eisenhower Elementrary school. I want to be a teacher when I grow up."

WOW! A teacher! Imagine that! I still cry every time I read it. That was the best present I have ever received. It came straight from her tranquil heart. This profound understanding and value of the true meaning of the Christmas season holds even more significance when the fact she is Jewish is factored in. It makes the book and it's author even more special.

She gave me the celebration to cry and reflect shortly after that, as well. On Dec. 28th, she wrote: "Dear Maryann, I really do miss you a whole lot and I want to spend a lot more time together then we usually do. We hope you had a nice Christmas with your family. Me and Noah really love you a whole lot. Since I have been trying to call you, I will write you a letter insted. Me and Noah really love you very much!!. Happy New Year!! Lot's of Love, Hannah and Noah Schwartz."

Knowing her sentiments verifies my purpose on this planet. It makes me proud to be a part of such a special development. If you ever ponder the age old question "What is my purpose?," just spend time with Hannah and you'll discover it. She has reassured me that I am exactly where I am meant to be. This is why I am here. If I ever forget, I re-read the special sentiments she immortalized on paper. And I know you've heard it before but now you know it too, she really is beautiful!

Epilogue

Now you see why I love being around the youth and innocence and beauty of children. They all provide me with a purpose on this Earth.

Each child is unique. No two have ever been alike and no two will ever be alike. Three of the greatest challenges of a parent or educator should be: First to accept their differences. Next, to appreciate their differences. And finally, to celebrate their differences. I celebrate the opportunity to explore each and every difference and discover the treasure buried within each child.

Children are like a precious gem. Some need polished a little more than others so their true beauty can shine for all to see. If children came with a treasure map with X marking the spot in which to uncover their inner potential, it would be convenient but dull. Following the trail that children leave for those around them is the best journey on which anyone can venture. It is filled with mystery, adventure, excitement, and dangers. When you get to the X, you know what the outcome is. It is a life. Do this for a child and you'll get more than any bounty you could set out for. What more could you want? What better treasure is there? It is priceless.

I am one of the lucky ones. I've found something I enjoy and have loved every minute of it. How could you not love, learn and appreciate a job working with children? Well, maybe if you are intolerant of bodily fluids, sticky hugs, head lice and other childhood maladies; you can't appreciate dandelions, need big miracles before celebrating, throw away old purses, shoes and make up cases, and have less than 100 ideas of what one can do with the cardboard tube from paper towels, this line of work isn't for you. But if you can, you are truly blessed because children will touch your heart and soul, and enhance your life.

I hope you've appreciated my lessons learned and that you have learned a few lessons yourself.

Just when I think I've seen it all and heard it all, another child comes along with still another lesson just waiting to be learned. So I'll keep living and learning. Isn't life great!

About the Author

MaryAnn Aikins-Rager has a degree in Pedology, which is the study of children. She has continued her studies through classes at Indiana University of Pennsylvania and Mt. Aloysius College. She has also logged endless hours of workshops and self study in her pursuit toward self-awareness and self-improvement.

She has written many other heartwarming stories, one of which was published in the Small Town Life Magazine. When she is not writing, she is teaching and learning from children in a preschool in rural Pennsylvania. She has worked, in one capacity or another, with children for over 25 years.

MaryAnn also enjoys sharing her experiences through public speaking. You may contact her at: uranaturalwoman@yahoo.com to schedule her to speak at your next event.

She has had the privilege of holding positions which has enabled her to mentor teachers and parents both professionally and personally.

Her skills, talents, experiences and knowledge continue to be highly respected and sought by colleagues and parents.